D1797351

Trend Horses

Trend Horses
Form Breakers for the Jumps 2008–2009

Andrew Mount

A **RACING POST** company

With thanks to...

Julian Brown and the team at Raceform, Bill and Janet for their proof-reading skills, Simon Nott for his contribution to this book and Jug Of Punch, who powered up the Cheltenham hill to win by five lengths after touching 289-1 in running.

Published in 2008 by Raceform Ltd
Compton, Newbury, Berkshire, RG20 6NL

Copyright © Andrew Mount 2008

The right of Andrew Mount to be identified as the author of this work has been asserted by him in accordance with the Copyright, Designs and Patents Act 1988.

All rights reserved. No part of this publication may be reproduced, stored in a retrieval system, or transmitted in any form or by any means, electronic, mechanical, photocopying, recording, or otherwise, without the prior written permission of the publishers.

A catalogue record for this book is available from the British Library.

ISBN 978-1-905153-92-3

Designed by Fiona Pike

Printed by Creative Print and Design, Wales

Contents

ABOUT THE AUTHOR   6

INTRODUCTION – WHAT ARE TREND HORSES?   7

COURSE DESCRIPTIONS/STATISTICS   9

A-Z OF TREND HORSES   13

GLOSSARY   119

INDEX   120

About the Author

ANDREW MOUNT is a professional gambler and leading racing advisor.
He has written (or co-written) several best-selling books about horseracing
including...

SprintLine 2002: incorporating the effects of the draw (with Graham Wheldon
and David Renham)
Trend Horses: Form Breakers for the Jumps and All-Weather Flat (with Peter
Stavers)
Form-Breakers for the Flat
Trend Horses: Form Breakers for the Jumps
Trend Horses: Drawn2win (with David Renham)
Trend Horses for the Jumps 2005 & All-weather Flat 2004-2005
Trend Horses for the Flat & Summer Jumps 2005
Trend Horses: Form Breakers for the Jumps 2005-2006
Trend Horses: Form Breakers for the Flat 2006
Trend Horses: Form Breakers for the Jumps 2006-2007
Trend Horses: Form Breakers for the Flat 2007
Trend Horses: Form Breakers for the Jumps 2007/08
Trend Horses: Form Breakers for the Flat 2008

His weekly Trend Horses column can be found on the GG.com website and he
also writes for Raceform Update.

Andrew can be contacted via email (Andrew@trendhorses.plus.com)
and can often be found in the Canary Wharf Sports Exchange
(www.canarywharfsports.com) pressing buttons like a lunatic.

Introduction
What Are Trend Horses?

Trend Horses are racehorses that have shown a strong preference for a certain set of race conditions. My aim is to uncover these patterns in order to identify potentially profitable bets.

Noticeable preferences may include one or more of the following: the need for a particular distance or going, for a small or large field, for a very recent outing or a long absence between races, for a certain class of race, for a flat or undulating course, or for a right-handed or left-handed track.

This book contains over 165 such horses but if I could pick just ten to follow this coming Jumps season I'd opt for these ...

BESHABAR
CORNAS
INGHWUNG
KENZO III
MALJIMAR
MOKUM
NENUPHAR COLLONGES
NEPTUNES COLLONGES
SURFACE TO AIR
TIDAL BAY

Once again, I'll be producing a free-to-read weekly Trend Horses column for the GG.com website this season, as well as giving daily selections on my Trend Horses Pro service and late selections on Trend Horses Live.

Best of luck

Andrew Mount

ANDREW MOUNT'S
TREND HORSES
PRO

Follow Andrew's 'Trend Horses' analysis on a daily basis by subscribing to **Trend Horses Pro**, **exclusive** to **GG.COM**

Trend Horses Pro subscribers will be able to access an exclusive preview of each day's racing via the website and email. The new service includes, within the cost, each day's **selected bets texted to your mobile phone** so you won't miss out

As a further incentive to sign up, Trend Horses Pro subscribers will receive the Trend Horses Live bets (see below) free of charge
To subscribe visit www.gg.com and click on Trend Horses Pro from the Tipping Features menu
FROM ONLY £99

SIGN UP FOR LAST MINUTE TIPS
WITH TREND HORSES LIVE!

Andrew occasionally receives 'insider information' or advises late bets as a result of non-runners, going changes etc. Text the words **GG THL** to **80806** to receive these SMS tips (average 3/4 per week) direct to your mobile phone

To stop the service, text the words **GG THL STOP** to 80806

GG.COM

COURSE DESCRIPTIONS

Course	Description
Aintree	Two left-handed courses. Grand National circuit, 2m2f, is flat and has huge fences with drop on landing side and a long run-in. Mildmay Course, 1m3f, flat with conventional fences, is sharper than the hurdles course. 13.19% of chase runners fell or unseated on the Mildmay course last season. A massive 46.51% of chase runners fell or unseated on the Grand National course.
Ascot	Right-handed, galloping, last mile mainly uphill, with stiff fences. Circuit 1m5f. Approximately 7.98% of runners fell or unseated their riders on the chase course last season (five-year figure = 8.04%).
Ayr	Left-handed, mainly flat. Circuit 1m4f. 11.86% of chase runners fell or unseated last term (five-year figure = 11.03%).
Bangor	Left-handed, sharp and flat with a long run-in. Circuit 1m4f. 6.17% fell or unseated last term (five-year figure = 7.48%).
Carlisle	Right-handed, undulating, stiff and galloping. Circuit 1m5f. 4.78% of chase runners fell or unseated last season (five-year figure = 4.28%).
Cartmel	Left-handed, sharp and undulating, with a four-furlong run-in for chases. Circuit 1m. Just 4.08% of chase runners fell or unseated during the 2007/2008 season, as compared to a five-year average of 6.67%.
Catterick	Left-handed, sharp and undulating, suiting handy types. Circuit 1m3f. 10.98% of chase runners fell or unseated last season (five-year average = 12.27%).
Cheltenham (old)	Left-handed, galloping, undulating and testing track with stiff fences. Circuit 1m4f.
Cheltenham (new)	Left-handed, galloping, undulating and testing track with stiff fences. Circuit 1m4½f.8.09% fell or unseated on the above two courses combined last term, as compared to a five-year average of 11.14% (figures do not include cross-country races).
Chepstow	Left-handed and undulating. Going can be very testing. Circuit 1m7f. 4.72% of chase runners fell or unseated last season (five-year average = 7.78%).
Doncaster	Left-handed, galloping, generally flat. Heavy ground rare. Circuit 2m. 4.58% of chase runners fell or unseated last season (five-year average = 12.05%).

Exeter Right-handed and undulating. Stiff test of stamina. Circuit 2m. 8.60% of chase runners fell or unseated last season (five-year average = 9.31%).

Fakenham Left-handed, sharp, undulating. Circuit 1m. 9.09% of chase runners fell or unseated last season (five-year average = 10.22%).

Folkestone Right-handed undulating oval of 1m2f. 4.26% of chase runners fell or unseated last season (five-year average = 5.18%).

Fontwell Left-handed hurdle course and figure-of-eight chase course. Ground can be testing. Circuit 1m. 9.56% of chase runners fell or unseated last season (five-year average = 7.51%).

Haydock Left-handed, flat and galloping. Chase course now on hurdles track and with portable fences. Suits gallopers but new course sharper than the old track. Circuit 1m4f. 3.79% of chase runners fell or unseated last season (five-year average = 6.49%).

Hereford Right-handed, sharpish and generally flat. Circuit 1m4f. 7.87% of chase runners fell or unseated last season (five-year average = 7.87%).

Hexham Left-handed, severe and undulating, placing emphasis on stamina. Circuit 1m4f. 8.45% of chase runners fell or unseated last season (five-year average = 8.19%).

Huntingdon Right-handed, flat and galloping. Circuit 1m4f. 9.86% of chase runners fell or unseated last season (five-year average = 10.70%).

Kelso Left-handed and undulating. Hurdles course of 1m1f is sharp, more so than 1m3f chase track, which has 2f run-in. 10.17% of chase runners fell or unseated last season (five-year average = 12.88%).

Kempton Right-handed triangular circuit of 1m5f, practically flat. 8.37% of chase runners fell or unseated last season (five-year average = 8.19%)

Leicester Right-handed and undulating, placing emphasis on stamina. Circuit 1m6f. 10.57% of chase runners fell or unseated last season (five-year average = 10.94%).

Lingfield Left-handed, undulating and sharp. Chase circuit 1m5f, hurdles run on flatter course. 4.52% of chase runners fell or unseated last season (five-year average = 6.59%).

Ludlow Right-handed. Chase course flat with sharp bends, circuit 1m4f. Hurdles track 150y longer, slightly undulating with easier bends. 8.11% of chase runners fell or unseated last season (five-year average = 8.66%).

Market Rasen	Right-handed oval, slightly undulating. Circuit 1m2f. 8.86% of chase runners fell or unseated last season (five-year average = 7.89%).
Musselburgh	Right-handed, virtually flat track with sharp turns. Circuit 1m3f. 10.53% of chase runners fell or unseated last season (five-year average = 10.35%).
Newbury	Left-handed, flat and galloping. Circuit 1m7f. 10.44% of chase runners fell or unseated last season (five-year average = 6.61%).
Newcastle	Left-handed, with uphill finish. Going can be very testing. Circuit 1m6f. 14.18% of chase runners fell or unseated last season (five-year average = 9.79%).
Newton Abbot	Left-handed oval, sharp with short run-in. Circuit 1m2f. 6.77% of chase runners fell or unseated last season (five-year average = 7.31%).
Perth	Right-handed and flat, with tight bends. Chase course has long run-in. Circuit 1m2f. 8.31% of chase runners fell or unseated last season (five-year average = 8.54%).
Plumpton	Left-handed, undulating, sharp. Circuit 1m1f. 15.93% of chase runners fell or unseated last season (five-year average = 11.94%).
Sandown	Right-handed with stiff uphill finish. Circuit 1m5f. 5.29% of chase runners fell or unseated last season (five-year average = 6.59%).
Sedgefield	Left-handed, undulating oval, sharp bends. Circuit 1m2f. 8.04% of chase runners fell or unseated last season (five-year average = 7.59%).
Southwell	Left-handed oval, approx 1m round, with six portable fences. Outside half of jumps course used in summer. 12.82% of chase runners fell or unseated last season (five-year average = 11.91%).
Stratford	Left-handed flat and sharp, with short finishing straight. Circuit 1m2f. 9.30% of chase runners fell or unseated last season (five-year average = 12.17%).
Taunton	Right-handed oval, on the sharp side with short run in. Circuit 1m2f. A massive 16.08% of chase runners fell or unseated last season (five-year average = 13.64%).
Towcester	Right-handed with last mile uphill. Very testing. Circuit 1m6f. 13.83% of chase runners fell or unseated last season (five-year average = 12.89%).

Uttoxeter	Left-handed with some undulations. Hurdle course is inside chase course. Circuit 1m3f. 4.73% of chase runners fell or unseated last season (five-year average = 7.98%).
Warwick	Left-handed with tight turns and short run-in. Circuit 1m5f. 5.94% of chase runners fell or unseated last season (five-year average = 6.18%).
Wetherby	Left-handed oval, with easy bends. Circuit 1m4f. 7.83% of chase runners fell or unseated last season (five-year average = 10.89%).
Wincanton	Right-handed rectangular circuit. Mainly flat. Circuit 1m3f. 11.90% of chase runners fell or unseated last season (five-year average = 11.36%).
Worcester	Left-handed 1m5f oval, flat with long straights and easy turns. 6.06% of chase runners fell or unseated last season (five-year average = 6.49%).

A-Z of Trend Horses

(all horses' records correct as of 31 August 2008)

ACAMBO (GER)
7yo gr g (D Pipe)

Race type	Hdl: 1135011P66 (4-10)
	Chs: 1F (1-2)
Conclusion:	he is a classy hurdler and made a winning start to his chase career.
Distance	2m-2m1f: 1135011P16 (5-10)
	2m3f-2m4f: 6F (0-2)
Conclusion:	all his wins have come at trips of about 2m.
Going	Good to firm or faster: 15 (1-2)
	Good: 016F (1-4)
	Good to soft: 1116 (3-4)
	Soft: 3P (0-2)
	Heavy: no runs
Conclusion:	he seems best on good to soft or faster going.
Fresh	First two runs or when rested for five weeks+: 11011P61F (5-9)
	Others: 356 (0-3)
Conclusion:	he runs especially well when fresh.
Headgear	Visor: 0 (0-1)
Conclusion:	he ran poorly when tried in a visor, finishing 23rd in the 2006 County Hurdle at the Cheltenham Festival.

Summary of ideal conditions Combine good to soft or faster going with running fresh (first two runs each season or when rested for five weeks or longer thereafter), when not wearing headgear, and his record becomes: 111161F (5-7), improving to: 11111 (5-5) at 2m-2m1f only.

AIR FORCE ONE (GER)
6yo ch g (C J Mann)

Race type	Hdl: F5112 (2-5)
	Chs: 6112511 (4-7)
Conclusion:	he was a useful hurdler and developed into a top class chaser last term, landing a Grade 1 novice event at the Punchestown Festival on his final outing.
Distance	2m: F (0-1)
	2m4f-2m5f: 116 (2-3)
	2m6f+: 52112511 (4-7)
Conclusion:	he needs a trip of at least 2m4f.

Going	Good to firm or faster: no runs
	Good: 1211 (3-4)
	Good to soft: 2615 (1-4)
	Soft: F511 (2-4)
	Heavy: no runs
Conclusion:	he has yet to race on extremes of going.
Course	Cheltenham: 525 (0-3)
Conclusion:	he jumped indifferently when fifth of 11 in the 2008 Royal & SunAlliance Chase and might prove best at tracks other than Cheltenham.
Fresh	Seasonal debuts: 56 (0-2)
Conclusion:	he is likely to need his first run of the season.

Summary of ideal conditions When racing over a distance of 2m4f or further, aside from seasonal debuts, his record is: 112112511 (6-9), with two of the three defeats coming at the Cheltenham Festival.

ALBERTAS RUN (IRE)
7yo b g (Jonjo O'Neill)

Race type	NHF: 110 (2-3)
	Hdl: 14111 (4-5)
	Ch: 121113 (4-6)
Conclusion:	he has an excellent strike-rate to date.
Distance	2m-2m1f: 11011 (4-5)
	2m4f-2m6f: 1412 (2-4)
	3m+: 11113 (4-5)
Conclusion:	he seems best at 3m or further.
Going	Good to firm or faster: no runs
	Good: 0112113 (4-7)
	Good to soft: 11 (2-2)
	Soft: 111 (3-3)
	Heavy: 41 (1-2)
Conclusion:	he is fully effective on good or softer going (he is untried on anything faster).
Jockey	Tony Dobbin: 0 (0-1)
	Noel Fehily: 1141 (3-4)
	A P McCoy: 11112113 (6-8)
	R Walsh: 1 (1-1)
Conclusion:	he has an excellent strike-rate for Tony McCoy.

Summary of ideal conditions He rarely runs a bad race and now has a career record of: 11014111121113 (10-14). From left to right: 1st, 1st, 15th of 23 – unsuited by fast ground, though not disgraced, in the 2006 Champion bumper, 1st, 4th – jumped poorly on first try beyond 2m (heavy going), 1st, 1st, 1st, 1st, 2nd – beaten by the useful Tidal Bay, 1st, 1st, 1st – landed the 2008 Royal & SunAlliance Chase, and 3rd – possibly found that the race (at the Aintree Festival) came too soon after his Cheltenham success.

ALDERBURN
9yo b g (H D Daly)

Race type	NHF: 283 (0-3)
	Hdl: 713362 (1-6)
	Chs: 41F17BP1153033 (4-14)
Conclusion:	he has a superior strike-rate over fences.
Going	Good to firm or faster: 23 (0-2)
	Good: 837241F1BP15033 (3-15)
	Good to soft: 671 (1-3)
	Soft: 133 (1-3)
	Heavy: no runs
Conclusion:	he has won on a soft surface but he seems best on good or faster going.

Field size (chase runs only)

	12 or more runners: 47P1303 (1-7)
	11 or fewer runners: 1F1B153 (3-7)
Conclusion:	he runs best in small fields.
Fresh	Seasonal debuts: 274P5 (0-5)
Conclusion:	he has yet to win first time out.
Track	Left-handed: 3247B1033 (1-9)
	Right-handed: 2837361F1P153 (3-13)
	Figure-of-eight: 1 (1-1)
Conclusion:	he has a moderate strike-rate on left-handed tracks.

Summary of ideal conditions Apart from seasonal debuts, his chase record reads: 1F17B113033 (4-11), improving to: 1F113 (3-5) when racing right-handed.

ANDREAS (FR)

8yo b g (P F Nicholls)

Race type	Hdl: 0F1 (1-3)
	Ch: 11F126F33331F74621 (5-18)
Conclusion:	he has winning form over hurdles and fences.
Distance	2m-2m2f: 0F11F1261F33331F74621 (6-21)
	2m3f+: no runs
Conclusion:	all his runs have taken place at trips of about 2m.
Going	Good to firm or faster: 113 (2-3)
	Good: F11F3F7621 (3-10)
	Good to soft: F26314 (1-6)
	Soft/heavy: 03 (0-2)
Conclusion:	he's best on a fast surface – his win in the 2007 Grand Annual Chase at the Cheltenham Festival came on officially 'good to soft' going but the final time of the race suggests that it was riding much quicker.
Time of year	October-February: F2613337 (1-8)
	March-May: 011F1F31F4621 (5-13)
Conclusion:	he won a weak handicap hurdle at Ludlow on 22 February 2006 but his other wins have come in the spring.

Summary of ideal conditions Combine hurdle or chase starts with racing on good or faster going (including that 2007 Grand Annual run) and his record becomes: F1111F331F7621 (6-14), improving to: 111F31F621 (5-10) during the March-May period.

ARDAGHEY (IRE)

9yo b/br g (N A Twiston-Davies)

Race type	NHF: 14 (1-2)
	Hdl: 41 (1-2)
	Ch: 36P21UF01P062166P0PF9 (3-21)
Conclusion:	he's effective over hurdles and fences.
Fresh (absence since last race)	
	42 days or longer: 113P11210 (5-9)
	35-41 days: no runs
	34 days or less: 4462UF0P0666PPF9 (0-16)
Conclusion:	he runs especially well when fresh.
Class	1: 6UP0626P0F (0-10)
	2: 4F016P9 (1-7)
	3 or lower: 1413P211 (4-8)
Conclusion:	he has yet to win in Class 1 company.

Field size   15 or more runners: 4UF0P060PF9 (0-11)
                   12-14 runners: P11P (2-4)
                   11 or fewer runners: 1413622166 (3-10)
Conclusion: he seems best in small fields.

Summary of ideal conditions When running fresh (after a break of five weeks or longer) his record reads: 113P11210 (5-9). From left to right: 1st, 1st, 3rd – entitled to need the experience on his chase debut in a race won by Star De Mohaison, P – pulled up (saddle slipped), 1st, 1st, 2nd – far from disgraced when nine lengths behind Simon in the 2007 Skybet Chase (Class 1), 1st, and 10th of 15 – unsuited to the big field and probably outclassed in the Grade 3 Racing Post Chase.

BAGAN (FR)

9yo b/br g (M Todhunter)

Race type   Hdl: 4111025 (3-7)
                  Chs: 14213181PP6 (4-11)
Conclusion: he is effective over hurdles and fences.

Distance   2m-2m2f: 4213 (1-4)
                  2m3f-2m5f: 111025141 (5-9)
                  3m+: 18PP6 (1-5)
Conclusion: he seems best at trips of about 2m4f (the 3m chase that he won
                  at Newbury in December 2007 was an uncompetitive and slowly
                  run affair).

Going   Good to firm: no runs
                  Good: 41102438P6 (2-10)
                  Good to soft: 112111P (5-7)
                  Soft: 5 (0-1)
                  Heavy: no runs
Conclusion: he seems best on good to soft going.

Summary of ideal conditions Combine a distance of 2m3f-2m5f with good or good to soft going and his record becomes: 1110214131 (6-10), improving to: 1111 (4-4) on good to soft going only.

BALLYFITZ

8yo b g (N A Twiston-Davies)

Race type	Hdl: 111271152 (5-9)
	Chs: U (0-1)
Conclusion:	his sole chase outing saw him unseat his rider after a series of blunders.
Distance	2m4f-2m7f: 127 (1-3)
	3m+: 1U11152 (4-7)
Conclusion:	he is best at 3m or further.
Going	Good or faster: 1U52 (1-4)
	Good to soft: 111 (3-3)
	Soft: 127 (1-3)
	Heavy: no runs
Conclusion:	Seems best on good to soft or softer going
Class	Grade 1: no runs
	Grade 2: 5 (0-1)
	Grade 3: 7 (0-1)
	Others: 11U12112 (5-8)
Conclusion:	he has yet to win above Listed level.

Summary of ideal conditions When racing over hurdles below Grade 3 level his record reads: 1112112 (5-7), improving to: 111 (3-3) at 3m or further on good to soft or softer going.

BATTLECRY

7yo b/br g (N A Twiston-Davies)

Race type	NHF: 13 (1-2)
	Hdl: FP29P13 (1-7)
	Chs: 1P52214332 (2-10)
Conclusion:	he is developing into a high-class chaser, having finished runner-up in a Grade 2 contest for novices on his final outing last term, but will need to improve his jumping if he is to progress further.
Distance	2m-2m2f: 13F12 (2-5)
	2m3f-2m6f: P2913P52 (1-8)
	3m+: P14332 (1-6)
Conclusion:	his 2m wins came in low class contests and he is likely to prove best at 3m or further.
Going	Good to firm or faster: 112 (2-3)
	Good: PP132 (1-5)
	Good to soft: 13P293543 (1-9)
	Soft: F2 (0-2)
	Heavy: no runs

Conclusion:	he seems best on good or faster going.
Track	Flat: 1P2P11P52142 (4-12)
	Significant undulations: 3F93233 (0-7)
Conclusion:	his four wins have come on flat courses (Worcester, Perth, Wetherby and Doncaster) and a Cheltenham record of: 3F933 (0-5) suggests that he is best avoided on testing tracks.
Field size	12 or more runners: F29 (0-3)
	10-11 runners: 13PP1132 (3-8)
	9 or fewer runners: 3P3 (0-3)
	7 or fewer runners: 15224 (1-5)
Conclusion:	all his wins have come in single-figure fields.

Summary of ideal conditions When racing on good to soft or faster going his record reads: 13P29P131P5214332 (4-17). These figures can be improved to: P11P12 (3-6) when only considering his flat-track runs on good or faster going.

BESHABAR (IRE)
6yo ch g (P F Nicholls)

Race type	Hdl: 2151 (2-4)
Conclusion:	his four runs under National Hunt Rules have taken place over hurdles but he is regarded as a potential future chase star.
Distance	2m3f-2m5f: 2151 (2-4)
Conclusion:	he is fully effective at about 2m4f but should stay 3m in time.
Going	Good: 1 (1-1)
	Good to soft: 215 (1-3)
	Soft/heavy: no runs
Conclusion:	his impressive Grade 3 Sandown win on his final start for Nick Williams came on good going but he is expected to prove best with some cut in the ground.

Summary of ideal conditions He made huge strides in just four outings for Nick Williams during the 2007-2008 season, finishing runner-up at 66-1 in a Newbury novices' hurdle before scoring at Exeter (evens) and Sandown (9-1). He has since changed hands for a not inconsiderable sum and is likely to prove Cheltenham Festival material for champion trainer Paul Nicholls.

BIBLE LORD (IRE)
7yo ch g (Andrew Turnell)

Race type	Hdl: 0 (0-1)
	Chs: 6211496140 (3-10)
Conclusion:	he's best over fences.
Distance	2m-2m2f: 0 (0-1)
	2m3f-2m5f: 21114 (3-5)
	3m+: 64960 (0-5)
Conclusion:	his best efforts have come at around 2m4f.
Going	Good or faster: 0 (0-1)
	Good to soft: 6214614 (2-7)
	Soft: 09 (0-2)
	Heavy: 1 (1-1)
Conclusion:	his sole start on ground faster than good to soft resulted in a comprehensive defeat, though it did come over a trip beyond his best (3m1f).
Field size (chase runs only)	
	12 or more runners: 649640 (0-6)
	11 or fewer runners: 2111 (3-4)
Conclusion:	he has yet to prove his effectiveness in a big field when racing over fences.

Summary of ideal conditions When racing over fences his record is: 6211496140 (3-10), improving to: 2111 (3-4) in fields of 11 or fewer runners, with all four runs taking place over a trip of about 2m4f.

BIG ROB (IRE)
9yo b g (B G Powell)

Race type	NHF: 5 (0-1)
	Hdl: 6P4231 (1-6)
	Chs: 112FFU221PPP04P6921PP (4-21)
Conclusion:	he is effective over hurdles and fences.
Distance	2m-2m1f110y: 56122 (1-5)
	2m2f-2m7f: P41FFU221PPP4P69311P (4-20)
	3m+: 02P (0-3)
Conclusion:	he seems best at trips short of 3m.
Going	Good to firm or faster: 1461 (2-4)
	Good: P12FF20932 (1-10)
	Good to soft: 561UPP1P (2-8)
	Soft/heavy: 422PPP (0-6)
Conclusion:	he prefers good to soft or faster going.

Track   Flat: 5P4112U221PP0469211 (5-19)
            Undulating: 6FF2PP3PP (0-9)
Conclusion: he performs best on flat tracks – his wins coming at Newbury,
            Wetherby and Huntingdon (three times).
Field size (chase runs only)
            12 or more runners: FP069PP (0-7)
            10-11 runners: FUP (0-3)
            9 or fewer runners: 112221P4P21 (4-11)
Conclusion: all his chase wins have come in single-figure line-ups.
Summary of ideal conditions When racing over fences in fields of nine or fewer
runners his record reads: 112221P4P21 (4-11). His small-field chase record can be
improved to: 11211 (4-5) if we only consider his runs on flat tracks, below 3m and
on good to soft or faster going.

BLACK HILLS
9yo b g (J A Geake)
Race type   NHF: 32 (0-2)
            Hdl: 1388 (1-4)
            Chs: 32321222100196988 (3-17)
Conclusion: the majority of his wins have come over fences.
Distance   2m-2m2f100y: 321388323 (1-9)
            2m3f-2m6f110y: 8212210019988 (3-13)
            3m+: 6 (0-1)
Conclusion: although not disgraced (he finished a 50-1 sixth of 15) he didn't
            seem to stay 3m in the 2008 Racing Post Chase at Kempton.
Track (chase runs only)
            Left-handed: 2832200998 (0-10)
            Right-handed: 3138322121168 (3-13)
Conclusion: he has yet to win on a left-handed track.
Field size (chase runs only)
            12 or more runners: 0096988 (0-7)
            11 or fewer runners: 3232122211 (3-10)
Conclusion: he performs best in small fields.
Summary of ideal conditions When racing over fences in fields of 11 or fewer
runners his record becomes: 3232122211 (3-10), improving to: 2122211 (3-7) in
handicaps of 2m3f-2m6f110y. All three wins took place on right-handed tracks, on
ground ranging from good to firm through to soft.

BLAEBERRY

7yo b m (Miss E C Lavelle)

Race type	Hdl: 2P42134146324110 (4-16)
	Chs: 113F (2-4)
Conclusion:	she is effective over hurdles and fences.
Distance	2m-2m2f: 2P423 (0-5)
	2m3f-2m5f110y: 13424111130F (5-12)
	2m6f+: 146 (1-3)
Conclusion:	she needs a trip of at least 2m3f.
Time of year	March-October: 134132411130F (5-13)
	November-February: 2P42461 (1-7)
Conclusion:	she tends to peak in spring/summer (her only win outside this period came on 1 November).
Class	1: 440 (0-3)
	2: 63F (0-3)
	3: 2P343111 (3-8)
	4: 421121 (3-6)
Conclusion:	she has yet to win above Class 3 level.

Summary of ideal conditions Combine a distance of 2m3f or further with running during the period from March to October and her record becomes: 134132411130F (5-13), improving to: 131321113F (5-10) when competing below Class 1 level.

BLANDINGS CASTLE

7yo ro g (Nick Williams)

Race type	Hdl: 90850981736 (1-11)
	Chs: 11451606 (3-8)
Conclusion:	he is effective over hurdles and fences.
Distance	2m-2m2f: 90850176114510 (4-14)
	2m3f-2m5f110y: 936 (0-3)
	2m6f+: 8 (0-1)
Conclusion:	he is best at about 2m.
Going	Good to firm or faster: 09114 (2-5)
	Good: 9858731560 (1-10)
	Good to soft: 0 (0-1)
	Soft/heavy: 61 (1-2)
Conclusion:	he seems effective on any going.
Course	Newton Abbot: 9508111416 (4-10)
	Others: 089736560 (0-9)
Conclusion:	he is a Newton Abbot course expert.
Class	Handicaps: 59173611451606 (4-14)
	Non-handicaps: 90808 (0-5)

Conclusion: all his wins have come in handicap company.
Headgear Visor: 08 (0-2)
Conclusion: he ran poorly when tried in a visor.
Summary of ideal conditions When running in handicaps at Newton Abbot his record becomes: 111416 (4-6), with the first defeat excusable as he was injured after stumbling three out. He is capable of running well fresh, having twice scored on his seasonal reappearance.

BRAVE VILLA (FR)
9yo b g (M Sheppard)
Race type Hdl: 060210620U90 (1-12)
Chs: 0F0032114115P156P234F (5-21)
Conclusion: he is best over fences.
Distance 2m-2m110y: 00210620U0311115P15624F (6-23)
2m1f-2m3f100y: F90024P3 (0-8)
2m4f+: 60 (0-2)
Conclusion: he struggles to stay much beyond 2m.
Field size (chase runs)
12 or more runners: 0F00345P (0-8)
8-11 runners: 121156P24 (3-9)
7 or fewer runners: 1134 (2-4)
Conclusion: he's a front-runner and is best able to dominate when racing in small fields.
Course Wincanton: 5F (0-2)
Conclusion: he has yet to impress over Wincanton's tricky fences.
Summary of ideal conditions When racing in chases of 11 or fewer runners at 2m-2m100y his record is: 111115624F (5-10). All these wins took place on good to soft or softer going.

BRIERY FOX (IRE)
10yo ch g (H D Daly)
Race type NHF: 1 (1-1)
Hdl: 413 (1-3)
Ch: 421021843B4U62225 (2-17)
Conclusion: he is effective over hurdles and fences.
Going Good or faster: 11102B4625 (3-10)
Good to soft: 321843U22 (1-9)
Soft/heavy: 44 (0-2)
Conclusion: he runs best on fast ground.

Field size (chase starts only)

12 or more runners: 083BU6225 (0-9)

8-11 runners: 4142(1-4)

7 or fewer runners: 2124 (1-4)

Conclusion: he has yet to win in a big field.

Summary of ideal conditions When racing on good or faster going his record is: 111024625 (3-9), improving to: 1112 (3-4) if we knock out his chase runs in fields of 12 or more runners.

BRING ME SUNSHINE (IRE)

7yo ch g (C L Tizzard)

Race type   NHF: 344 (0-3)

Hdl: 4161PP476 (2-9)

Chs: 1P841P1P (3-8)

Conclusion: he is effective over hurdles and fences.

Distance   2m-2m2f: 3441P6 (1-6)

2m3f-2m5f: 4161P47411 (4-10)

2m6f+: PP8P (0-4)

Conclusion: he seems best at trips short of 2m6f.

Field size   9 or more runners: 34446PPP47846P (0-14)

8 or fewer runners: 1111P1 (5-6)

Conclusion: all his wins have come in small fields.

Fresh (absence since last race)

42 days or longer: 341P144 (2-7)

28-41 days: P (0-1)

27 days or less: 4416PP781P61 (3-12)

Conclusion: he is capable of running well after a long break but doesn't have to be fresh.

Summary of ideal conditions When racing in fields of eight or fewer runners his record becomes: 1111P1 (5-6). All these wins came on good to soft or softer going at 2m-2m5f.

BRONSON F'SURE

9yo b g (C T Pogson)

Race type   Chs: 459524U11184521 (4-15)

Conclusion: all his runs have taken place over fences.

Distance   2m-2m5f110y: 495484 (0-6)

2m6f-2m7f110y: 5U (0-2)

3m+: 2111521 (4-7)

Conclusion: he needs a trip of at least 3m.

Going	Good to firm or faster: 112 (2-3)
	Good: 5181 (2-4)
	Good to soft: 945 (0-3)
	Soft/heavy: 4524U (0-5)
Conclusion:	he is best on good or faster going.

Summary of ideal conditions Combine a distance of 3m or further with running on good or faster going and his record becomes: 11121 (4-5). All these wins took place over fences in March/April.

CARIBOU (FR)
6yo b g (O Sherwood)

Race type	Hdl: 141 (2-3)
	Ch: 322411P8221P (3-12)
Conclusion:	he is effective over hurdles and fences.
Going	Good or faster: 2PP (0-3)
	Good to soft: 322 (0-3)
	Soft/heavy: 141241181 (5-9)
Conclusion:	he handles good to soft but prefers soft or heavy going.
Track	Left-handed: 43281 (1-5)
	Right-handed: 11211P22P (4-9)
	Figure-of-eight: 4 (0-1)
Conclusion:	he has a superior strike-rate on right-handed tracks.

Summary of ideal conditions When racing on good to soft or softer going his record reads: 141324118221 (5-12), improving to: 1121122 (4-7) on right-handed tracks only.

CHARACTER BUILDING (IRE)
8yo ch g (J J Quinn)

Race type	NHF: 322 (0-3)
	Hdl: 24121 (2-5)
	Chs: 412P3 (1-5)
Conclusion:	he's effective over hurdles and fences.
Distance	2m-2m2f: 322 (0-3)
	2m3f-2m6f: 241241 (2-6)
	3m-3m2f110y: 13 (1-2)
	4m+: 2P (0-2)
Conclusion:	he ran subsequent Irish Grand National winner Butler's Cabin close when runner-up in the 4m1f National Hunt Chase at the 2007 Cheltenham Festival and appears suited by a test of stamina.

Going	Good to firm or faster: 1P (1-2)
	Good: 22 (0-2)
	Good to soft: 2 (0-1)
	Soft: 3224113 (2-7)
	Heavy: 4 (0-1)
Conclusion:	his fast-ground win came in a weak race at Sedgefield and he is likely to prove best on good or softer going.

Summary of ideal conditions When racing on good or softer going his record over obstacles stands at: 24214123 (2-8), improving to: 12 (1-2) at 3m or further, with the latest defeat coming in Denman's Hennessy – his only run during the 2007/2008 National Hunt season.

CLOUDY LANE
8yo b g (D McCain Jnr)

Race type	NHF: 21 (1-2)
	Hdl: F21121 (3-6)
	Chs: 361201U51116 (5-12)
Conclusion:	he has winning form over hurdles and fences.
Distance	2m-2m2f: 21F (1-3)
	2m3f-2m6f: 211136 (3-6)
	3m-3m1f: 2121511 (4-7)
	3m2f: 1 (1-1)
	3m4f+: 0U6 (0-3)
Conclusion:	he has proved disappointing when tried over extreme trips and is likely to prove best at around the 3m-3m2f mark.
Going	Good or faster: 13U16 (2-5)
	Good to soft: F2161 (2-5)
	Soft: 211251 (3-6)
	Heavy: 2101 (2-4)
Conclusion:	he seems happiest on good to soft or softer going.
Fresh	Seasonal debuts: 2F35 (0-4)
	Second run: 1261 (2-4)
	Third or subsequent runs: 11211201U116 (7-12)
Conclusion:	he has yet to win first time out.

Course	Aintree (Grand National): 6 (0-1)
	Aintree (Mildmay): 3 (0-1)
	Ayr: 1 (1-1)
	Bangor: 26 (0-2)
	Cheltenham: 1 (1-1)
	Doncaster: 1 (1-1)
	Fairyhouse: U (0-1)
	Haydock: 111051 (4-6)
	Hexham: F (0-1)
	Newcastle: 12 (1-2)
	Sedgefield: 2 (0-1)
	Southwell: 1 (1-1)
	Uttoxeter: 2 (0-1)

Conclusion: he twice ran poorly on tight courses (Aintree and Bangor) during the 2006/2007 season and seems best on galloping tracks.

Summary of ideal conditions When racing over hurdles or fences at 2m4f or further his record becomes: 21121361201U51116 (8-17), improving to: 2111121111 (8-10) if we throw out his runs on tight tracks and those at 3m4f or further. His lack of size, stamina and experience accounted for his 2008 Grand National defeat and, hopefully, his connections will give Aintree a miss from now on, despite their obvious affinity with the place.

COACH LANE

7yo b g (Miss Venetia Williams)

Race type	Hdl: 53823146381 (2-11)
	Chs: U211418956342161 (5-16)

Conclusion: he has a near one-in-three strike-rate over fences.

Distance	2m-2m1f: 53821438U211134211 (6-18)
	2m2f+: 364895661 (1-9)

Conclusion: he narrowly landed a fast-ground hurdle over 2m4f at Towcester in May 2008 but his other wins have come at about 2m.

Going	Good or faster: 8561 (1-4)
	Good to soft: 568U2861 (1-8)
	Soft: 324319321 (2-9)
	Heavy: 311414 (3-6)

Conclusion: he runs especially well on soft or heavy going.

Field size (chase runs only)

> 12 or more runners: 961 (1-3)
> 8-11 runners: U4853426 (0-8)
> 6-7 runners: 2 (0-1)
> 5 or fewer runners: 1111 (4-4)

Conclusion: the majority of his chase wins have come in very small fields.

Summary of ideal conditions When racing over fences at 2m-2m1f his record is: U211134211 (5-10), improving to: 1111 (4-4) in fields of five or fewer runners.

COPPER BAY (IRE)

6yo b g (A King)

Race type	Hdl: 3345 (0-4)
	Chs: P3211FP5P1P7 (3-12)
Conclusion:	all his wins have come over fences.
Distance	2m-2m2f: 3345P3211FPP (2-12)
	2m3f-2m4f: 517 (1-3)
	2m4f110y+: P (0-1)
Conclusion:	he is effective from 2m-2m4f.
Going	Good to firm or faster: no runs
	Good: 4211P1P7 (3-8)
	Good to soft: 53 (0-2)
	Soft/heavy: 33PFP5 (0-6)
Conclusion:	his three wins came on officially good going.
Track	Left-handed: 35P32PP7 (0-8)
	Right-handed: 3411F51P (3-8)
Conclusion:	all his wins have come on right-handed tracks – at Leicester (twice) and Market Rasen.

Summary of ideal conditions When racing right-handed on good or faster going his record becomes: 4111P (3-5), with the non-completion coming over Wincanton's tricky fences.

CORNAS (NZ)

6yo b g (Nick Williams)

Race type	NHF: 76 (0-2)
	Hdl: 5512 (1-4)
Conclusion:	he showed some ability in bumpers when with Evan Williams and landed one of his four hurdle starts for Nick Williams last term.
Distance	2m-2m1f: 765512 (1-6)
Conclusion:	all his runs have come over trips of about 2m.
Going	Good to firm or faster: no runs

Good: 7512 (1-4)
Good to soft: 6 (0-1)
Soft: 5 (0-1)
Heavy: no runs

Conclusion: his sole win came on good going but he seemed to handle soft ground when fifth of 16 at Wincanton in March 2008.

Summary of ideal conditions Cornas has shown ability in all his hurdle starts to date, recording figures of: 5512 (1-4). From left-to-right: 5th — backed from 50-1 into 11-1 at Hereford where he might have placed but for a bad mistake, 5th — pulled too hard but not disgraced in a 16-runner line-up at Wincanton, 1st — accounted for Imperial Cup third Albinus and 14 others in a novice hurdle at Wincanton, and 2nd — no match for the progressive Woolcombe Folly when a 17-length second on his handicap debut at Stratford. Although yet to race beyond 2m1f he should stay further and, like most from this yard, can be followed blind this season.

DANCING DASI (IRE)

9yo b m (V R A Dartnall)

Race type	Hdl: 25553212521 (2-11)
Conclusion:	all her runs have taken place over hurdles.
Going	Good to firm: no runs
	Good: 1 (1-1)
	Good to soft: 252122 (1-6)
	Soft/heavy: 5535 (0-4)
Conclusion:	her best efforts have come on good or good to soft going.
Track	Left-handed: 555 (0-3)
	Right-handed: 25321221 (2-8)
Conclusion:	she tends to jump out to her right and has been kept to that direction for the majority of her 11 starts. Her three left-handed efforts all took place at Newbury where she was beaten by 19, 16 and 21 lengths.

Summary of ideal conditions When racing right-handed on good to soft or faster going her record becomes: 2521221 (2-7), with the sole unplaced effort excusable as she pulled too hard in a small field at Ascot (a run needed to qualify her for a handicap mark).

DICTUM (GER)
10yo ch g (Mrs Susan Nock)

Race type	Hdl: 214P387 (1-7)
	Chs: 35110R5 (2-7)
Conclusion:	he is effective over hurdles and fences.
Distance	2m-2m2f: 214P33517 (2-9)
	2m3f-2m5f: 810R5 (1-5)
Conclusion:	his latest win came at 2m4f but he might stay further.
Going	Good or faster: 4P (0-2)
	Good to soft: 2385057 (0-7)
	Soft: 3 (0-1)
	Heavy: 111R (3-4)
Conclusion:	he prefers heavy going.
Fresh	Seasonal debuts: 233R (0-4)
Conclusion:	he has yet to win first time out.

Summary of ideal conditions When racing on soft or heavy going his record reads: 1311R (3-5), improving to: 111 (3-3) if we ignore his seasonal debuts.

DOUBLE EAGLE
6yo b g (D McCain)

Race type	NHF: 19 (1-2)
	Hdl: 433123 (1-6)
	Chs: 31P (1-3)
Conclusion:	he has only once finished out of the frame when racing over jumps.
Distance	2m-2m2f: 19 (1-2)
	2m3f-2m4f: 1231 (2-4)
	2m4f110y-3m1f: 4333 (0-4)
	4m+: P (0-1)
Conclusion:	he has yet to win beyond 2m4f.
Going	Good or faster: 3 (0-1)
	Good to soft: 93P (0-3)
	Soft: 1431 (2-4)
	Heavy: 321 (1-3)
Conclusion:	his best efforts have come on soft or heavy going.
Track	Left-handed: 94331 (1-5)
	Right-handed: 11233P (2-6)
Conclusion:	he jumped out to his right when recording a first chase success at left-handed Ayr in February 2008 and is likely to prove best on right-handed tracks.

Summary of ideal conditions When racing right-handed at trips short of 4m his record is: 11233 (2-5). From left to right: 1st – won a Carlisle bumper by 23 lengths (8-1), 1st – won a 2m4f novice hurdle at Carlisle by four lengths (16-1), 2nd (of 16) – placed in Grade 3 company at Sandown (33-1), 3rd – probably needed the run on his 2007/2008 reappearance, and 3rd – far from disgraced behind Tidal Bay when 16-1 for his chase debut.

DREAM ALLIANCE
7yo ch g (P J Hobbs)

Race type	NHF: 42 (0-2)
	Hdl: 3116F5 (2-6)
	Chs: 1243612PUPP (2-11)
Conclusion:	he is effective over hurdles and fences.
Distance	1m5f-2m3f: 423 (0-3)
	2m4f-2m5f110y: 11 (2-2)
	2m6f-2m7f110y: 1U (1-2)
	3m+: 6F5243612PPP (1-12)
Conclusion:	he has a moderate strike-rate at 3m or further and might prove best at around 2m4f-2m6f.
Class	1: 62PPP (0-5)
	2: 51U (1-3)
	3: 312436 (1-6)
	4 or lower: 4211F (2-5)
Conclusion:	he has yet to win above Class 2 level.
Fresh	Seasonal debuts: 4252 (0-4)
Conclusion:	he might need his first run of the season.

Summary of ideal conditions Combine a distance of 2m4f or further with racing below Class 1 company, excluding seasonal debuts, and his record becomes: 11F124361U (4-10), improving to: 111U (3-4) at 2m4f-2m7f110y only.

EARTH PLANET (IRE)
6yo b g (P F Nicholls)

Race type	NHF: 123 (1-3)
	Hdl: 2526114 (2-7)
Conclusion:	he has reached a place in eight of his ten career starts (the fourth placing came in a handicap of 17 runners).
Distance	2m-2m2f110y: 123 (1-3)
	2m3f-2m5f110y: 252114 (2-6)
	2m6f+: 6 (0-1)
Conclusion:	his best efforts have come at about 2m4f but he might stay further.

Going	Good to firm or faster: no runs
	Good: 14 (1-2)
	Good to soft: 225261 (1-6)
	Soft: 31 (1-2)
	Heavy: no runs
Conclusion:	he has yet to race on extremes of going.
Field size	12 or more runners: 1256114 (3-7)
	11 or fewer runners: 232 (0-3)
Conclusion:	his three wins came in big fields.
Track	Left-handed: 13561 (2-5)
	Right-handed: 22214 (1-5)
Conclusion:	he has winning form on both left-handed and right-handed tracks.
Headgear	Tongue-tie: 114 (2-3)
	Without: 1232526 (1-7)
Conclusion:	he improved when a tongue tie was fitted.
Jockey	Ruby Walsh: 12114 (3-5)
	Others: 32526 (0-5)
Conclusion:	all his wins came when ridden by Ruby Walsh.

Summary of ideal conditions Earth Planet proved expensive and frustrating to follow after he scored by a short head in a Chepstow bumper on his racecourse debut – he lost six times in a row (usually at short odds after travelling strongly). The application of a tongue-tie brought about a change of fortune at Wincanton on 31 March 2008 where he simply hacked up under Ruby Walsh. His full record for Walsh now reads: 12114 (3-5).

EDMO YEWKAY (IRE)

8yo b/br g (T D Easterby)

Race type	Hdl: 612414P84F79 (2-12)
	Chs: 2431425421254P32494251314 (4-25)
Conclusion:	the majority of his wins have come over fences.
Distance	2m-2m2f110y: 612414P2441 (3-11)
	2m3f-2m5f110y: 84931242125432492513 4 (3-21)
	2m6f+: F745P (0-5)
Conclusion:	although a dual winner over an extended 2m4f he seems best over shorter trips these days – his last two wins coming at 2m and 2m3f.

Going	Good to firm or faster: 4 (0-1)
	Good: 61P54491 (2-8)
	Good to soft: 44479342225314 (1-14)
	Soft/Heavy: 218F212154P342 (3-14)
Conclusion:	he has winning form on ground ranging from good through to heavy.
Field size	12 or more runners: 612PF7932P94 (1-12)
	11 or fewer runners: 41484244125421543242 51314 (5-25)
Conclusion:	he's best in small fields (his only big-field win came in a 12-runner novices' hurdle back in November 2003).
Track	Left-handed: 61241P84F9243154124P3244251314 (6-30)
	Right-handed: 4742259 (0-7)
Conclusion:	he has yet to win on a right-handed track.
Track	Aintree: 44 (0-2)
	Ayr: 224 (0-3)
	Bangor: 3 (0-1)
	Carlisle: 59 (0-2)
	Catterick: 43 (0-2)
	Cheltenham: P (0-1)
	Chepstow: 2 (0-1)
	Doncaster: 191 (2-3)
	Haydock: 541 (1-3)
	Hexham: 2 (0-1)
	Huntingdon: 44 (0-2)
	Market Rasen: 7 (0-1)
	Newcastle: 61 (1-2)
	Perth: 2 (0-1)
	Sedgefield: F (0-1)
	Stratford: 8 (0-1)
	Towcester: 2 (0-1)
	Uttoxeter: P (0-1)
	Warwick: 243 (0-3)
	Wetherby: 41145 (2-5)
Conclusion:	he seems best on flat/galloping tracks – he hasn't won away from Doncaster, Haydock or Wetherby since November 2003.

Summary of ideal conditions Combine chase starts of 11 or fewer runners with a distance of 2m-2m5f110y and his record becomes: 241242154324251314 (4-18), improving to: 114511 (4-6) at Doncaster, Haydock or Wetherby only.

EL ZORRO

7yo b g (N B King)

Race type	Hdl: 118P (2-4)
Conclusion:	all his runs have taken place over hurdles.
Distance	2m: 1 (1-1)
	2m5f: 1 (1-1)
	2m6f+: 8P (0-2)
Conclusion:	he is unbeaten over trips short of 2m6f.
Going	Good or faster: 8 (0-1)
	Good to soft: 1 (1-1)
	Soft: P (0-1)
	Heavy: 1 (1-1)
Conclusion:	he is likely to prove best on slow going.
Fresh (absence since last race)	
	42 days or longer: 11 (2-2)
	41 days or less: 8P (0-2)
Conclusion:	he runs especially well when fresh.

Summary of ideal conditions El Zorro has only had four runs since leaving France (where he placed in all three starts over hurdles) but it seems likely that he'll prove best when fresh on good to soft or softer going – his record under such conditions being: 11 (2-2), with the wins coming at odds of 9-1 and 8-1.

ELUSIVE DREAM

7yo b g (P F Nicholls)

Race type	Hdl: 11421411 (5-8)
Conclusion:	he has an excellent strike-rate over jumps.
Going	Good or faster: 111411 (5-6)
	Good to soft: no runs
	Soft: 42 (0-2)
	Heavy: no runs
Conclusion:	he seems best on a sound surface.

Summary of ideal conditions When racing on good or faster going his record stands at: 111411 (5-6). He seems well suited to racing in small fields – four of his five wins over jumps have come in fields of eight or fewer runners and his seven Flat wins came in fields of ten or less.

ELVIS RETURNS
10yo b g (J M Jefferson)

Race type	NHF: 68 (0-2)
	Hdl: 2424 (0-4)
	Chs: 83221185P8612329 (3-16)
Conclusion:	he is best over fences.
Going	Good or faster: 2821 (1-4)
	Good to soft: 844186232 (1-9)
	Soft: 63215P9 (1-7)
	Heavy: 28 (0-2)
Conclusion:	he seems best on good to soft or faster going.
Time of year	Jan-Feb: 8382 (0-4)
	Mar-May: 22211619 (3-8)
	June-Sept: no runs
	Oct-Dec: 6842485P23 (0-10)
Conclusion:	all his wins have come in the spring.
Headgear	Cheekpieces: 6 (0-1)
Conclusion:	he ran poorly when tried in cheekpieces.

Summary of ideal conditions He tends to come good in the spring, recording figures of: 22211619 (3-8) from March to May, improving to: 2211 (2-4) when racing on good to soft or faster going without headgear.

ERIC'S CHARM (FR)
10yo b g (O Sherwood)

Race type	NHF: 115 (2-3)
	Hdl: 1132124P (3-8)
	Chs: F1216P12225PF1 (4-14)
Conclusion:	he's effective over hurdles and fences.
Going	Good to firm or faster: 2 (0-1)
	Good: 15131416P (4-9)
	Good to soft: 112F21P22PF1 (4-12)
	Soft/heavy: 215 (1-3)
Conclusion:	he seems to handle any going.
Fresh	Seasonal debuts: 11FPP (2-5)
Conclusion:	he won first time out in 2002/03 (in a weak Fontwell bumper) and in 2003/04 (when 2-5 favourite in a poor contest) but has run as though needing his reappearance in the last few seasons.

| **Track** | Left-handed: 15124F6PPF (2-10) |
| | Right-handed: 11312121P122251 (7-15) |

Conclusion: the majority of his wins have come on right-handed tracks.

Summary of ideal conditions When racing right-handed, excluding seasonal debuts, his record is: 11312121122251 (7-14).

FINGER ONTHE PULSE (IRE)

7yo b g (T J Taafe)

Race type	NHF: 1 (1-1)
	Hdl: F221312110UF (4-12)
	Chs: 3F2215 (1-6)

Conclusion: he is effective over hurdles and fences.

Distance	2m-2m2f: 1F2211 (3-6)
	2m3f-2m5f: 32110UF3F221 (3-12)
	3m+: 5 (0-1)

Conclusion: he seems best at 2m-2m5f.

Going	Good to firm: F (0-1)
	Good: 5 (0-1)
	Good to yielding: F23 (0-3)
	Yielding: 21U1 (2-4)
	Yielding to soft: 31 (1-2)
	Soft: 10 (1-2)
	Soft to heavy: 112 (2-3)
	Heavy: 2F2 (0-3)

Conclusion: he seems effective on most going types.

Fresh	First two runs each season or after a break of five weeks+:
	1F21110U3F15 (5-12)
	Others: 2132F22 (1-7)

Conclusion: he runs especially well when fresh.

| **Time of year** | Mar-Oct: F1211UF15 (4-9) |
| | Nov-Feb: 1221303F22 (2-10) |

Conclusion: the majority of his wins have come outside the winter months.

Summary of ideal conditions When racing over trips short of 3m his record reads: 1F221312110UF3F221 (6-18), improving to: F1111 (4-5) when running fresh from March to October.

FOREST PENNANT (IRE)
6yo b/br g (P F Nicholls)

Race type	NHF: 461 (1-3)
	Hdl: 231141 (3-6)
Conclusion:	he has a 50% strike-rate over hurdles and will no doubt make an impact if switched to fences this term.
Distance	2m-2m2f: 461 (1-3)
	2m3f-2m5f: 23114 (2-5)
	3m+: 1 (1-1)
Conclusion:	he has a good strike-rate at about 2m4f and seemed to improve for the step up to 3m1f on his final 2007/2008 start, landing a Listed Handicap hurdle from 21 rivals at the Aintree Festival.
Going	Good to firm or faster: no runs
	Good: 41 (1-2)
	Good to soft: 4121 (2-4)
	Soft: 3 (0-1)
	Heavy: 61 (1-2)
Conclusion:	he has winning form on ground ranging from good through to heavy.

Summary of ideal conditions When racing over 2m3f or further his record stands at: 231141 (3-6), with the latest defeat excusable as he found the combination of 2m4f and good ground an insufficient test of stamina.

FORGET THE PAST
10yo b g (M J P O'Brien)

Race type	Hdl: 352138 (1-6)
	Ch: 1121210331135140146P (8-20)
Conclusion:	he's effective over hurdles and fences.
Distance	2m4f-2m6f: 321122103111146 (7-15)
	3m-3m1f: 513154038 (2-9)
	3m2f+: 3P (0-2)
Conclusion:	he just about lasted 3m in novice company but seems best at 2m4f-2m6f.
Going	Good or faster: 335381 (1-6)
	Good to yielding: 6P (0-2)
	Yielding: 52100 (1-5)
	Yielding to soft: 13 (1-2)
	Soft: 221311 (3-6)
	Soft/heavy: 11 (2-2)
	Heavy: 144 (1-3)
Conclusion:	he seems best on slow going.

Class   Grade 1: 2123335404 (1-10)
                   Grade 2: 1111 (4-4)
                   Grade 3: 10 (1-2)
                   Others: 352113816P (3-10)
Conclusion: he won in Grade 1 company as a novice back in December 2004
                   but seems most effective at a lower level.

Summary of ideal conditions Combine a distance of 2m4f-2m6f with racing on
yielding to soft or softer going and his record becomes: 122131114 (5-9), improving
to: 11111 (5-5) when racing below Grade 1 level.

FROM DAWN TO DUSK
9yo b g (P J Hobbs)

Distance   2m-2m2f: 10 (1-2)
                   2m3f-2m6f: 98431112431131 (6-14)
                   3m+: 42 (0-2)
Conclusion: he seems best at trips below 3m.
Going   Good or faster: 11121231 (5-8)
                   Good to soft: 1431 (2-4)
                   Soft/heavy: 908434 (0-6)
Conclusion: he needs good to soft or faster going.
Time of year   Jan-Feb: 843 (0-3)
                   Mar-May: 1311112 (5-7)
                   June-Aug: no runs
                   Sep-Oct: 131 (2-3)
                   Nov-Dec: 90244 (0-5)
Conclusion: he has a poor record during the winter months.

Summary of ideal conditions When racing on good to soft or faster going his
record is: 111124311231 (7-12), improving to: 11111131 (7-8) at 2m-2m6f during
the period of March to October.

GONE TO LUNCH (IRE)
8yo ch g (J Scott)

Race type	Hdl: 211112352 (4-9)
	Chs: F (0-1)
Conclusion:	a point-to-point winner, he fell on his Rules debut (in the 2007 Christie's Foxhunter Chase at the Cheltenham Festival) before a string of good efforts over hurdles.
Going	Good to firm or faster: 1 (1-1)
	Good: 21112 (3-5)
	Good to soft: F352 (0-4)
	Soft/heavy: no runs
Conclusion:	he performs best on fast ground.

Summary of ideal conditions When racing over hurdles his record is: 211112352 (4-9), improving to: 2111122 (4-7) on good or faster going only, with the latest defeat by a neck. A trip of 3m or further is ideal.

GREEN GAMBLE (GB)
8yo gr g (D M Grissell)

Race type	NHF: 0 (0-1)
	Hdl: 76403220438P (0-12)
	Chs: 12523P5855P2111 (4-15)
Conclusion:	he is best over fences.
Distance	1m5f: 0 (0-1)
	2m-2m1f: 60322431523P88P5P111 (4-20)
	2m2f-2m3f: 7452 (0-4)
	2m4f+: 025 (0-3)
Conclusion:	he seems best at 2m-2m1f.
Going	Good to firm or faster: 715388 (1-6)
	Good: 4032422P5P5521 (1-14)
	Good to soft: 23P11 (2-5)
	Soft: 60 (0-2)
	Heavy: 7 (0-1)
Conclusion:	he seems best on good to soft or faster going.
Headgear	Blinkers: 5 (0-1)
Conclusion:	he ran poorly when tried in blinkers.

Summary of ideal conditions Combine chase starts of 2m-2m1f with good to soft or faster going, when not wearing headgear, and his record becomes: 1523P85P111 (4-11). All four wins came in fields of 11 or fewer runners and he seems best on sharp tracks such as Folkestone and Lingfield.

GUNGADU

8yo ch g (P F Nicholls)

Race type	Hdl: 3121273 (2-7)
	Chs: 1211F6115 (5-9)
Conclusion:	he was a useful hurdler but is even better over fences.
Track	Left-handed: 3127121F365 (3-11)
	Right-handed: 12111 (4-5)
Conclusion:	he has a superior strike-rate on right-handed tracks.
Field size	12 or more runners: 2F61 (1-4)
	10-11 runners: 71 (1-2)
	8-9 runners: 113 (2-3)
	7 or fewer runners: 3212115 (3-7)
Conclusion:	he had previously seemed best in small fields but proved that he could handle traffic by winning the 15-runner Racing Post Chase in February 2008.

Summary of his ideal conditions When racing right-handed his record is: 12111 (4-5), improving to: 111 (3-3) in fields of 11 or fewer runners.

GWANAKO (FR)

5yo b/br g (P F Nicholls)

Race type	Hdl: 1345 (1-4)
	Chs: 321 (1-3)
Conclusion:	he is effective over hurdles and fences.
Distance	2m-2m2f: 135 (1-3)
	2m3f-2m5f100y: 4321 (1-4)
	2m6f+: no runs
Conclusion:	he won at 2m on his British debut (he was unbeaten in five jumps outings in France) but his latest win came over an extended 2m5f and that sort of trip is likely to prove more suitable.
Going	Good to firm or faster: no runs
	Good: 14 (1-2)
	Good to soft: 35321 (1-5)
	Soft/heavy: no runs
Conclusion:	he has yet to race on extremes of going.
Track (UK runs only)	
	Left-handed: 13421 (2-5)
	Right-handed: 53 (0-2)
Conclusion:	he jumped out to his left when an odds-on flop in a graduation chase at right-handed Kempton last term and is likely to prove best on left-handed tracks.

Summary of ideal conditions Since joining current trainer Paul Nicholls his record reads: 1345321 (2-7), improving to: 13421 (2-5) on left-handed tracks.

HALCON GENELARDAIS (FR)
8yo ch g (A King)

Race type	Hdl: 211F413 (3-7)
	Chs: 111513P242 (4-10)
Conclusion:	he has a good strike-rate over hurdles and fences.
Distance	2m-2m5f: 21F (1-3)
	2m6f+: 141115113P3242 (6-14)
Conclusion:	he is best at 2m6f or further.
Going	Good or faster: 452 (0-3)
	Good to soft: 11F1P34 (3-7)
	Soft/heavy: 2111132 (4-7)
Conclusion:	the softer the going, the better he runs.

Summary of ideal conditions His UK record on good to soft or softer going reads: 211F1111133242 (7-14), improving to: 111132 (4-6) at 2m6f or further on soft/heavy going only, with the latest defeat by a head in the Welsh National when conceding 21lb to the winner (Miko De Beauchene).

HELENS VISION
5yo b m (Miss H Lewis)

Race type	NHF: 22114 (2-5)
	Hdl: 13P60400 (1-8)
Conclusion:	she had a good record in bumpers but has been disappointing since her hurdling debut.
Fresh (absence since last race)	
	42 days or longer: 2111 (3-4)
	28-41 days: 3P40 (0-4)
	27 days or less: 24600 (0-5)
Conclusion:	she runs especially well when fresh.

Summary of ideal conditions When rested for six weeks or longer her record reads: 2111 (3-4), with the sole defeat by a head when a 28-1 shot on her racecourse debut. All her wins came at 2m-2m1f and she seems effective on any going.

HENRY'S PRIDE (IRE)

8yo ch g (Mrs A M Thorpe)

Race type	NHF: 53 (0-2)
	Hdl: 8 (0-1)
	Chs: 2U23P6133615203P (2-16)
Conclusion:	all his wins have come over fences.
Distance	2m-2m6f: 538223 (0-6)
	3m-3m2f: U3P61615203 (2-11)
	3m4f+: 3P (0-2)
Conclusion:	he seems best at about 3m.
Going	Good to firm or faster: 13 (1-2)
	Good: 33520P (0-6)
	Good to soft: 36 (0-2)
	Soft: 582U36 (0-6)
	Heavy: 2P1 (1-3)
Conclusion:	he seems to handle any going but might prove best on a slow surface.
Fresh (absence since last race)	
	42 days or longer: 532P1103 (2-8)
	35-41 days: 6 (0-1)
	28-34 days: 82P (0-3)
	27 days or less: U236335 (0-7)
Conclusion:	he runs best when fresh.

Summary of ideal conditions Combine chase starts with running fresh (after a break of six weeks or longer) and his record becomes: 2P113 (2-5), with the non-completion excusable as he was badly hampered.

HERMANO CORDOBES (IRE)

8yo b g (P J Hobbs)

Race type	NHF: 0 (0-1)
	Hdl: 652PP543 (0-8)
	Chs: 13215 (2-5)
Conclusion:	he's best over fences.
Distance	2m-2m2f: 0 (0-1)
	2m3f-2m5f110y: 6P55 (0-4)
	2m6f-2m7f110y: 2P4312 (1-6)
	3m+: 315 (1-3)
Conclusion:	his most recent win (at Newton Abbot on 14 July 2008) came over an extended 3m2f and he probably needs at least 3m these days.

Going	Good to firm: P23 (0-3)
	Good: 53121 (2-5)
	Good to soft: 0645 (0-4)
	Soft/heavy: P5 (0-2)
Conclusion:	he prefers good or faster going.

Field size (chase runs only)

	12 or more runners: 5 (0-1)
	8-11 runners: 3 (0-1)
	7 or fewer runners: 121 (2-3)
Conclusion:	his jumping remains far from fluent and he is likely to prove best in small fields.

Summary of ideal conditions When racing over fences his record reads: 13215 (2-5), improving to: 1321 (2-4) on good or faster going.

HOWLE HILL (IRE)

8yo b g (A King)

Race type	Hdl: 1214500333025504 (2-16)
	Chs: 1114160P (4-8)
Conclusion:	he has a 50% strike-rate over fences.
Distance	2m-2m3f: 1214500333050111410P (6-20)
	2m4f-2m6f: 2546 (0-4)
Conclusion:	all his wins have come at 2m-2m3f.
Going	Good or faster: 15003330411116P (5-15)
	Good to soft: 21405540 (1-8)
	Soft: 2 (0-1)
	Heavy: no runs
Conclusion:	he is best on good or faster going.
Course	Aintree: 0 (0-1)
	Ascot: 16 (1-2)
	Cheltenham: 4555040 (0-7)
	Chepstow: 2 (0-1)
	Doncaster: 1 (1-1)
	Fontwell: 1 (1-1)
	Haydock: 0 (0-1)
	Huntingdon: 2 (0-1)
	Newbury: 30 (0-2)
	Sandown: 4P (0-2)
	Warwick: 1 (1-1)
	Wetherby: 13 (1-2)
	Wincanton: 13 (1-2)
Conclusion:	he has a poor record on tracks with stiff uphill finishes (e.g. Cheltenham and Sandown).

Summary of ideal conditions When racing over fences on good or faster going his record becomes: 11116P (4-6), improving to: 1111 (4-4) at 2m-2m3f on easy tracks.

ICE BUCKET (IRE)

8yo ch g (Miss H C Knight)

Race type	NHF: 360 (0-3)
	Hdl: 645 (0-3)
	Chs: 912346P5215 (2-11)
Conclusion:	he improved for the switch to fences.
Track	Left-handed: 6045935 (0-7)
	Right-handed: 3612465P21 (2-10)
Conclusion:	his best efforts have come on right-handed tracks.

Course (right-handed chase runs only)

	Hereford: 1 (1-1)
	Huntingdon: 1 (1-1)
	Huntingdon: 1 (1-1)
	Leicester: P5 (0-2)
	Market Rasen: 4 (0-1)
	Kempton: 2 (0-1)
	Sandown: 6 (0-1)
	Wincanton: 2 (0-1)
Conclusion:	he seems best on flat courses.
Fresh	Seasonal debuts: 3694 (0-4)
Conclusion:	he might need his first run of the season.

Summary of ideal conditions Aside from seasonal debuts, his right-handed chase record stands at: 126P521 (2-7), improving to: 1221 (2-4) if we discard his runs on stiff tracks (e.g. Sandown and Leicester). He has winning form on ground ranging from good through to soft and is effective from 2m4f-3m.

IDLE TALK (IRE)

9yo br g (D McCain Jnr)

Race type	Hdl: 141P (2-4)
	Chs: 1132426UUUU28U5750 (2-18)
Conclusion:	he is effective over hurdles and fences.
Class	1: 4P32426UUUU8U570 (0-16)
	2: 25 (0-2)
	3: 111 (3-3)
	4: 1 (1-1)
Conclusion:	he has yet to score at Class 1 level.

Field size (chase starts only)

> 16 or more runners: 46UUUU5750 (0-10)
> 12-15 runners: 1228 (1-4)
> 8-11 runners: U (0-1)
> 7 or fewer runners: 132 (1-3)

Conclusion: given his prominent running style and tendency to make mistakes, small fields are likely to suit best.

Summary of ideal conditions When racing below Class 1 level his record is: 11112 (4-5), with the sole defeat excusable as he found 2m4f on fast ground an inadequate test of stamina on his 2007/2008 reappearance.

IL DUCE (IRE)

8yo br g (A King)

Race type	NHF: 521 (1-3)
	Hdl: 221P12F60 (2-9)
	Chs: 1231PF2312PP2P (3-14)
Conclusion:	he is effective over hurdles and fences.
Distance	2m-2m2f: 52122 (1-5)
	2m3f-2m5f: 1120123F2312PP2 (4-15)
	2m6f-2m7f110y: 1P (1-2)
	3m+: PF6P (0-4)
Conclusion:	he is best at trips of about 2m4f.
Going	Good or faster: 52PF02312P (1-10)
	Good to soft: 221126131P2 (4-11)
	Soft/heavy: PF2P (0-4)
	Polytrack: 1 (1-1)
Conclusion:	he seems best on good to soft or faster going.
Class	1: P0F2PP2P (0-8)
	2: F63P (0-4)
	3: 21221231 (3-8)
	4 or lower: 521211 (3-6)
Conclusion:	he has yet to win above Class 3 level though did finish a close second in the Grade 3 (Class 1) Paddy Power Gold Cup at Cheltenham in November 2007.

Fresh (absence since last race)

> 35 days or longer: 522P260121F32PP (2-15)
> 34 days or less: 1211F3P21P2 (4-11)

Conclusion: he is capable of running well after a long break but doesn't have to be fresh.

Time of year	Jan-Feb: 226PF (0-5)
	Mar: 102P (1-4)
	Apr-May: 5P11312 (3-7)
	Jun-Aug: P (0-1)
	Sep-Oct: 2 (0-1)
	Nov: 22F32 (0-5)
	Dec: 11P (2-3)

Conclusion: the majority of his wins have come in the spring.

Chase runs by field size

	12 or more runners: 2PP2P (0-5)
	8-11 runners: 3 (0-1)
	7 or fewer runners: 1231PF21 (3-8)

Conclusion: his chase wins have come in small fields.

Summary of ideal conditions When racing from 2m3f-2m7f110y his record reads: 11201231F2312PP2P (5-17), improving to: 1120121312PP2 (5-13) on good to soft or faster going, with two of the unplaced efforts coming at the Cheltenham Festival.

I'M SUPREME (IRE)
6yo b g (P J Hobbs)

Race type	NHF: 5 (0-1)
	Hdl: 05200 (0-5)
	Chs: 51P15 (2-5)

Conclusion: he's best over fences.

Distance	2m-2m2f110y: 50 (0-2)
	2m3f-2m6f110y: 52005P (0-6)
	3m+: 115 (2-3)

Conclusion: he improved for the step up to 3m+.

Going	Good or faster: 200511 (2-6)
	Good to soft: 5 (0-1)
	Soft/heavy: 505P (0-4)

Conclusion: he prefers good or faster going.

Fresh Seasonal debuts: 500 (0-3)

Conclusion: he might need his first run of the season.

Summary of ideal conditions When racing over 3m or further his record reads: 115 (2-3), improving to: 11 (2-2) on good or faster going only. Both wins came on flat right-handed tracks.

INCORPORATION
9yo b g (Mrs L Williamson)

Race type	Hdl: P4P (0-3)
	Chs: 56P129357281371513225 (4-21)
Conclusion:	he has improved since switched to fences.
Distance	2m-2m2f110y: P51293721371513225 (4-18)
	2m3f-2m5f: 4P6P58 (0-6)
Conclusion:	he seems best at trips of around 2m, though hasn't yet encountered his preferred underfoot conditions when racing over longer trips.
Going	Good or faster: 4P29357835 (0-10)
	Good to soft: 6P7325 (0-6)
	Soft/heavy: P6121112 (4-8)
Conclusion:	he seems best on soft or heavy going.
Headgear	Cheekpieces: 129357281371513225 (4-18)
	Without headgear: P4P56P (0-6)
Conclusion:	his best efforts have come when wearing cheekpieces.

Summary of ideal conditions When racing on soft or heavy going his record in cheekpieces stands at: 121112 (4-6), with all the wins coming at a distance of about 2m after a break of 28 days or more.

INGHWUNG
6yo b m (O Sherwood)

Race type	NHF: 322 (0-3)
	Hdl: 411P1 (3-5)
Conclusion:	she showed useful form in bumpers but improved for the switch to hurdles.
Distance	2m-2m3f: 3223 (0-4)
	2m4f-2m6f110y: 11P1 (3-4)
	3m+: 4 (0-1)
Conclusion:	she needs at least 2m4f.
Going	Good to firm: 1 (1-1)
	Good: 1 (1-1)
	Good to soft: 31 (1-2)
	Soft/heavy: 3224P (0-5)
Conclusion:	all her wins have come on good to soft or faster going.

Summary of ideal conditions When racing over 2m4f or further her record becomes: 411P1 (3-5), improving to: 111 (3-3) on good to soft or faster going only.

IRISH RAPTOR (IRE)
9yo b/br g (N A Twiston-Davies)

Race type	Hdl: 84691 (1-5)
	Chs: PU31UU21217U786146526 (4-21)
Conclusion:	he's effective over hurdles and fences.
Distance	2m-2m5f110y: PU86372 (0-7)
	3m+: 491UU21271U18614656 (5-19)
Conclusion:	he needs a trip of at least 3m.
Going	Good or faster: U9718 (1-5)
	Good to soft: P81U2U616526 (2-12)
	Soft: 3U114 (2-5)
	Heavy: 4627 (0-4)
Conclusion:	he seems best on good to soft or softer going.
Field size (chase runs only)	
	12 or more runners: UU786652 (0-8)
	8-11 runners: 31U27146 (2-8)
	7 or fewer runners: PU121 (2-5)
Conclusion:	he is still inclined to make jumping errors and he is likely to prove best in small fields.

Summary of ideal conditions Combine chase starts of 3m or further with racing on good to soft or softer going, in fields of 11 or fewer runners, and his record becomes: 1UU21271146 (4-11), with the seventh place coming in a Grade 2 contest.

IRONSIDE (IRE)
9yo b g (C L Tizzard)

Race type	Hdl: P235P878 (0-8)
	Chs: 3P24P2P152852P5101P462PP (3-24)
Conclusion:	he's best over fences.
Going	Good or faster: PP8PP (0-5)
	Good to soft: P28P62 (0-6)
	Soft/heavy: 235873P24P1525251014P (3-21)
Conclusion:	he prefers soft or heavy going.
Fresh (absence since last race)	
	42 days or longer: P3P82P (0-6)
	22-41 days: 532P285P (0-8)
	15-21 days: 274P862P (0-8)
	8-14 days: P1525104P (2-9)
	7 days or less: 1 (1-1)
Conclusion:	all his wins came after a recent outing (13, eight and six days).

Headgear Blinkers: 1528585101P462PP (3-16)
      Without headgear: P235P873P24P2P2P (0-16)
Conclusion: he seems best in blinkers.
Course (chase runs only)
      Bangor: 4 (0-1)
      Chepstow: 21 (1-2)
      Exeter: PP (0-2)
      Folkestone: 6 (0-1)
      Haydock: 3P5 (0-3)
      Lingfield: P (0-1)
      Plumpton: 511 (2-3)
      Taunton: 2P (0-2)
      Towcester: P (0-1)
      Warwick: 24250 (0-5)
      Wincanton: 82P (0-3)
Conclusion: two of his three wins came at Plumpton and both were preceded
      by an unplaced effort at Warwick where he has a poor record (his
      latest runner-up effort there was a comprehensive 52-length
      defeat).
Field size (chase runs only)
      12 or more runners: P58PP (0-5)
      11 or fewer runners: 3P242P12525101462PP (3-19)
Conclusion: he's a front-runner and is best able to dominate when racing in
      small fields.
Summary of ideal conditions Combine blinkered chase starts with running on soft
or heavy going, after a recent outing (21 days or less), and his record becomes:
1551014P (3-8), improving to: 1114P (3-5) if we discard his runs at Warwick and
those in fields of 12 or more runners.

JACK THE GIANT (IRE)

6yo b g (N J Henderson)
Race type Hdl: 123211 (3-6)
      Chs: 111361 (4-6)
Conclusion: he has winning form over hurdles and fences and has only once
      finished outside of the first three places.
Distance 2m-2m2f: 12321113611 (6-11)
      2m3f+: 1 (1-1)
Conclusion: the majority of his runs have taken place at about 2m but he does
      stay further.

Going	Good to firm or faster: 211 (2-3)
	Good: 132161 (3-6)
	Good to soft: 11 (2-2)
	Soft/heavy: 3 (0-1)
Conclusion:	he is suited by good to soft or faster going. His 2007 Champion Chase third came on ground officially described as soft (good to soft in places) but Raceform rated it as good going.
Field size	12 or more runners: 12331 (2-5)
	11 or fewer runners: 2111611 (5-7)
Conclusion:	as a front-runner he is likely to prove best suited to racing in small fields.
Fresh	First two runs each season or after a break of five weeks+: 123111311 (6-9)
	Other runs: 261 (1-3)
Conclusion:	he runs especially well when fresh.

Summary of ideal conditions When racing on good to soft or faster going (including that Champion Chase third) his record is: 123211136111 (7-12), improving to: 123111311 (6-9) when fresh.

JIGSAW DANCER (IRE)

6yo ch g (Andrew Turnell)

Race type	Non-handicap hurdles: 0BU4 (0-4)
	Handicap hurdles: P31113 (3-6)
Conclusion:	he improved for the switch to handicap company.
Distance	2m-2m2f110y: 0PU4P3111 (3-9)
	2m3f+: 3 (0-1)
Conclusion:	all his wins came at about 2m but he does stay further.
Going	Good or faster: no runs
	Good to soft: 0UP313 (1-6)
	Soft/heavy: B411 (2-4)
Conclusion:	he runs especially well on soft or heavy going.
Track	Left-handed: 1 (1-1)
	Right-handed: 0BU4P3113 (2-9)
Conclusion:	he won his only left-handed start (at Bangor) but jumped out to his right and is likely to prove best when racing clockwise.

Summary of ideal conditions When racing in handicap company his record is: P31113 (3-6), with the non-completion excusable as his rider pulled him up after losing his irons.

KALAHARI KING (FR)

7yo b/br g (Ferdy Murphy)

Race type	Hdl: 3142431 (2-7)
Conclusion:	he has yet to finish out of the frame when racing over jumps.
Distance	2m-2m1f: 14243 (1-5)
	2m4f: 31 (1-2)
Conclusion:	he is effective from 2m-2m4f and might stay further.
Going	Good or faster: 3431 (1-4)
	Good to soft: 124 (1-3)
	Soft/heavy: no runs
Conclusion:	he has yet to race on soft or heavy going.

Summary of ideal conditions When racing over hurdles his record is: 3142431 (2-7). He progressed rapidly last season after his debut third in a Musselburgh maiden hurdle – finishing a 40-1 fourth in the Grade 1 Supreme Novices' Hurdle at Cheltenham and landing the Aon Hurdle over 2m4f at the Punchestown Festival. There should be more to come this term, especially if he's stepped up in trip.

KALCA MOME (FR)

10yo b g (P J Hobbs)

Race type	Hdl: 218151100 (4-9)
	Chs: 12141319552718427F62310641282061305686 (8-38)
Conclusion:	he is effective over hurdles and fences.
Going	Good or faster: 211439571F306636 (3-16)
	Good to soft: 2115807062280568 (2-16)
	Soft: 81512424101 (4-11)
	Heavy: 1112 (3-4)
Conclusion:	the best of his recent efforts have come on soft or heavy going.
Class	1: 95030008 (0-8)
	2: 45841F1641282613566 (4-19)
	3: 2185113127127062 (5-16)
	4: 1121 (3-4)
Conclusion:	he has yet to win in Class 1 company.

Summary of ideal conditions Combine chase starts with racing on soft or heavy going, below Class 1 company, and his record becomes: 124214121 (4-9), improving to: 112 (2-3) on heavy going only. All his wins have come over trips short of 2m4f.

KEENAN'S FUTURE (IRE)

7yo ch g (Ian Williams)

Race type	
	NHF: 3 (0-1)
	Hdl: 11U (2-3)
	Chs: B3R15146613F (3-12)
Conclusion:	he won both his completed starts over hurdles and is a multiple chase winner.
Going	
	Good to firm or faster: no runs
	Good: 31546F (1-6)
	Good to soft: 1R11 (3-4)
	Soft: 3B63 (0-4)
	Heavy: 1U (1-2)
Conclusion:	he is likely to prove best on good to soft or softer going.
Track	Left-handed: 31U15146613 (4-11)
	Right-handed: 1B3RF (1-5)
Conclusion:	he has failed to complete the course in three of his last four starts on right-handed tracks and is likely to prove best when racing left-handed.
Field size	12 or more runners: 315463F (1-7)
	11 or fewer runners: 1UB3R1161 (4-9)
Conclusion:	he seems best in small fields, his chase wins coming in fields of eight, nine and eight runners.

Summary of ideal conditions When racing over hurdles, or on left-handed chase tracks, his record becomes: 11U15146613 (5-11), improving to: 11U11613 (5-8) on ground slower than good.

KEMPSKI

8yo b g (R Nixon)

Race type	
	NHF: 5906 (0-4)
	Hdl: P22P00P5423634P5326113644P30781P4 (3-33)
	Chs: R6UR (0-4)
Conclusion:	he's best over hurdles.
Distance	2m-2m2f: 59062055376R4 (0-13)
	2m4f: P2P2634P113441P (3-15)
	2m5f+: P043R266P308U (0-13)
Conclusion:	all his wins have come at 2m4f.

Going (hurdle starts only)

Good or faster: 03 (0-2)

Good to soft: P22P (0-4)

Soft: P0536P36407 (0-11)

Heavy: 2P4234536114P814 (3-16)

Conclusion: he has placed form on a variety of going but all his wins have come on a heavy surface.

Field size (hurdle starts only)

12 or more runners: 2P0036P2663078P4 (0-16)

11 or fewer runners: P2P542345311344P1 (3-17)

Conclusion: he's a front-runner and is better able to dominate when racing in small fields.

Course (hurdle starts only)

Ayr: P22523611P14 (3-12)

Carlisle: P43P534 (0-7)

Haydock: P (0-1)

Kelso: P0266378 (0-8)

Newcastle: 434 (0-3)

Perth: 00 (0-2)

Conclusion: he has yet to win away from Ayr.

Summary of ideal conditions When racing over hurdles at Ayr his record reads: P22523611P14 (3-12), improving to: 22111 (3-5) at 2m4f on heavy going. From left-to-right: 2nd – placed at 50-1 in maiden company on only his second start over hurdles, 2nd – found only one too good when a blinkered first-time 14-1 shot in novice company, 1st (12-1), 1st (7-1) and 1st 20-1. The three wins all came in handicap company, in small fields and after a very recent outing (eight, eight and seven days).

KENZO III (FR)

10yo ch g (N J Henderson)

Distance   2m-2m2f: no runs

2m3f-2m5f110y: 1P1U (2-4)

3m+: 1P32P5 (1-6)

Conclusion: his first win came over a sharp 3m (at Ludlow) but he has since seemed best over shorter trips.

Going   Good or faster: 32P (0-3)

Good to soft: 1P1P1U5 (3-7)

Soft/heavy: no runs

Conclusion: all his wins have come on good to soft going and he has yet to race on anything slower.

Fresh (absence since last race)

56 days or longer: 1131 (3-4)

42-55 days: PU (0-2)

28-41 days: P (0-1)

27 days or less: P25 (0-3)

Conclusion: he runs especially well when fresh.

Summary of ideal conditions Best when fresh, his seasonal debut figures read: 111 (3-3) and he'll again be hard to beat on his reappearance.

KILBEGGAN BLADE

9yo b g (T R George)

Race type

NHF: 50 (0-2)

Hdl: 07053080332 (0-11)

Chs: 2134111P441P0P (5-14)

Conclusion: he's best over fences.

Going (chase starts only)

Good or faster: 2344P (0-5)

Good to soft: 1 (1-1)

Soft: 1131 (3-4)

Heavy: 1P4P (1-4)

Conclusion: he needs good to soft or softer going.

Fresh (absence since last race)

28-41 days: 0PP (0-3)

27 days or less: 0703080131111320 (5-16)

Conclusion: all his wins have come when returned to the track within four weeks of his previous outing.

Summary of ideal conditions Combine chase starts with running on good to soft or softer going, when returned to the track within four weeks of his previous outing, and his record becomes: 1111410 (5-7), with the latest defeat coming at the Cheltenham Festival.

KINGS EURO (IRE)

8yo b g (Tim Vaughan)

Race type

Hdl: 2121 (2-4)

Chs: 112P (2-4)

Conclusion: he's effective over hurdles and fences.

Distance

2m4f-2m6f110y: 12111 (4-5)

3m+: 22P (0-3)

Conclusion: he has twice gone close over 3m but all his wins have come over shorter trips.

Going	Good or faster: 2P (0-2)
	Good to soft: 212 (1-3)
	Soft/heavy: 111 (3-3)
Conclusion:	he is unbeaten on soft or heavy going.

Summary of ideal conditions When racing on good to soft or softer going his record reads: 211112 (4-6), improving to: 1111 (4-4) at trips below 3m.

KINGS ROCK

7yo ch g (J R Holt)

Race type	Non-handicap hurdles: 95000267 (0-8)
	Handicap hurdles: 430212P64611FP (3-14)
Conclusion:	all his wins have come in handicap hurdles.
Distance	2m-2m2f110y: 9500042266 (0-10)
	2m3f-2m4f110y: 3026P4 (0-6)
	2m5f-2m6f110y: 111 (3-3)
	3m+: 7FP (0-3)
Conclusion:	he is unbeaten when racing over trips of about 2m6f.
Going	Good or faster: 3261P (1-5)
	Good to soft: 95000012P4F (1-11)
	Soft: 461 (1-3)
	Heavy: 267 (0-3)
Conclusion:	he seems effective on any going.

Fresh (absence since last race)

	42 days or longer: 9676 (0-4)
	28-41 days: 426 (0-3)
	15-27 days: 02024 (0-5)
	14 days or less: 50031P11FP (3-10)
Conclusion:	all his wins came after a very recent outing.

Summary of ideal conditions When racing in handicap hurdles after a recent outing (within four weeks) his record becomes: 3021P411FP (3-10), improving to: 111 (3-3) at 2m5f-2m6f110y only.

KNIGHTON LAD (IRE)

8yo b g (A King)

Race type	NHF: 732 (0-3)
	Hdl: B425112190 (3-10)
Conclusion:	he has a 30% strike-rate over hurdles.
Distance	2m-2m2f: 732 (0-3)
	2m3f-2m7f: B42 (0-3)
	3m+: 5112190 (3-7)
Conclusion:	he needs a trip of at least 3m.
Going	Good to firm: 21 (1-2)
	Good: 73B49 (0-5)
	Good to soft: 1 (1-1)
	Soft/heavy: 25120 (1-5)
Conclusion:	he has winning form on fast and heavy going.
Fresh (absence since last race)	
	42 days or longer: 732B121 (2-7)
	35-41 days: 10 (1-2)
	34 days or less: 4295 (0-4)
Conclusion:	he runs especially well when fresh.

Summary of ideal conditions When racing at 3m or further his record reads: 5112190 (3-7), improving to: 121 (2-3) when rested for six weeks or more, with the sole defeat by half a length.

KNOWHERE (IRE)

10yo b g (N A Twiston-Davies)

Race type	Hdl: 11 (2-2)
	Chs: P11F22380U135P16UP (4-18)
Conclusion:	he's effective over hurdles and fences.
Distance	2m3f-2m5f110y: 11P11F22813P (5-12)
	3m-3m1f110y: 301 (1-3)
	3m2f+: U56UP (0-5)
Conclusion:	he won the 2008 Cotswold Chase over 3m1f110y at Cheltenham but that was a slowly run affair and he's likely to prove best over shorter trips.
Fresh (absence since last race)	
	First two runs or after a break of six weeks+: 111101316 (6-9)
	Others: PF2238U5PUP (0-11)
Conclusion:	he runs especially well when fresh.

Class	Grade 1: 306 (0-3)
	Grade 2: 1P21 (2-4)
	Grade 3: 528J35PUP (0-9)
	Others: 1111 (4-4)

Conclusion: he might not be up to winning at Grade 1 level.

Summary of ideal conditions When running fresh (first two starts each season or after a break of six weeks or more) his record becomes: 111101316 (6-9), improving to: 1111131 (6-7) when racing below Grade 1 level. His jumping still gives cause for concern, so he might prove best in small fields.

LA VECCHIA SCUOLA (IRE)

4yo b f (J S Goldie)

Race type	Hdl: 54321531495110 (4-14)
Conclusion:	she has a good strike-rate over hurdles.
Distance	2m-2m1f: 54215110 (3-8)
	2m1f110y-2m4f: 3314 (1-4)
	2m4f110y-2m5f110y: 9 (0-1)
	3m+: 5 (0-1)
Conclusion:	she won a slowly run novice hurdle over 2m4f at Musselburgh but her other wins have come at about 2m.
Going	Good to firm or faster: 54 (0-2)
	Good: 31510 (2-5)
	Good to soft: 531491 (2-6)
	Soft: 2 (0-1)
	Heavy: no runs
Conclusion:	she seems happiest on good or good to soft going.
Field size	12 or more runners: 54215314950 (2-11)
	10-11 runners: 3 (0-1)
	9 or fewer runners: 11 (2-2)
Conclusion:	her two most recent wins have come in single-figure line-ups, as did her four wins on the Flat.

Summary of ideal conditions When racing over a distance of 2m-2m1f her hurdles record becomes: 54215110 (3-8), improving to: 11 (2-2) when racing in fields of nine or fewer runners.

LENNON (IRE)

8yo b/br g (J Howard Johnson)

Distance	2m-2m2f: 21210149111174136244 (8-20)
	2m3f-2m5f: 2 (0-1)
Conclusion:	he was an odds-on failure when tried over 2m4f at Market Rasen in November 2005 and has since raced exclusively at trips of about 2m.
Going	Good to firm or faster: 1 (1-1)
	Good: 210911143244 (4-12)
	Good to soft: 116 (2-3)
	Soft: 2471 (1-4)
	Heavy: 2 (0-1)
Conclusion:	he seems best on good to soft or faster going.
Track	Flat: 21212191111413624 (8-17)
	Significant undulations: 0474 (0-4)
Conclusion:	he prefers flat tracks.

Summary of ideal conditions If we discard his runs on soft or heavy going and those on tracks with significant undulations (e.g. Cheltenham and Sandown) his record becomes: 21119111113624 (8-14).

LODGE LANE (IRE)

7yo b g (V R A Dartnall)

Race type	NHF: 110 (2-3)
	Hdl: 1101 (3-4)
Conclusion:	he has a 75% strike-rate over hurdles.
Distance	2m-2m2f: 110 (2-3)
	2m3f-2m5f: 11 (2-2)
	3m+: 01 (1-2)
Conclusion:	he is effective over a variety of trips.
Going	Good to firm or faster: no runs
	Good: 1 (1-1)
	Good to soft: 001 (1-3)
	Soft: 1 (1-1)
	Heavy: 11 (2-2)
Conclusion:	he's unbeaten on soft or heavy going.
Track	Left-handed: 11010 (3-5)
	Right-handed: 11 (2-2)
Conclusion:	he is unbeaten on right-handed tracks.

Summary of ideal conditions He is somewhat quirky – he hung right and almost ran off the track when tenth of 24 in the 2007 Champion Bumper – but if we discard his two runs at the Cheltenham Festival his record becomes: 11111 (5-5).

LORD HENRY (IRE)
9yo b g (P J Hobbs)

Race type	NHF: 4 (0-1)
	Hdl: 1137910 (3-7)
	Chs: 11F6F421P32 (3-11)
Conclusion:	he is effective over hurdles and fences.
Track	Left-handed: 7910F6P3 (1-8)
	Right-handed: 411311F4212 (5-11)
Conclusion:	he has a superior strike-rate on right-handed tracks.
Class	1: 7904P32 (0-7)
	2: F2 (0-2)
	3: 11311F61 (5-8)
	4 or lower: 41 (1-2)
Conclusion:	he has yet to win above Class 3 level but did finish runner-up in a Grade 2 (Class 1) contest on his final outing last term.

Summary of ideal conditions When racing right-handed over jumps his record reads: 11311F4212 (5-10), improving to: 1111F21 (5-7), if we discard his runs in Class 1 company and those on heavy ground.

LORD RYEFORD (IRE)
8yo br g (T R George)

Race type	NHF: 47 (0-2)
	Hdl: 08157321 (2-8)
	Chs: 2P4111400P13 (4-12)
Conclusion:	he is effective over hurdles and fences.
Going	Good to firm: 711 (2-3)
	Good: 471211403123 (4-12)
	Good to soft: 085P0P (0-6)
	Soft/heavy: 4 (0-1)
Conclusion:	he prefers good or faster going.
Field size	12 or more runners: 470857P440303 (0-13)
	11 or fewer runners: 12111P121 (6-9)
Conclusion:	he has yet to win in a big field.

Summary of ideal conditions Combine hurdle or chase starts with racing in fields of 11 or fewer runners, on good or faster going, and his record becomes: 12111121 (6-8). His wins came over distances ranging from 2m to 2m5f110y.

MADISON DU BERLAIS (FR)
7yo b g (D E Pipe)

Distance	2m-2m2f: 31113381153 (5-11)
	2m3f-2m5f: U64173 (1-6)
	3m+: 425F (0-4)
Conclusion:	five of his six UK wins have come at about 2m but he stays further.
Going	Good or faster: 1133342F (2-8)
	Good to soft: 3575 (0-4)
	Soft/heavy: U18641131 (4-9)
Conclusion:	he handles most conditions but four of his last five wins have come on soft or heavy going.
Fresh (absence since last race)	
	28 days or longer: U338245F (0-8)
	27 days or less: 1113641153172 (6-13)
Conclusion:	he runs best after a recent outing.
Track	Flat: U3113113142F (5-12)
	Significant undulations: 186455735 (1-9)
Conclusion:	he has a superior strike-rate on easy tracks – his last four wins coming at Newbury (twice), Southwell and Warwick.

Summary of ideal conditions When returning to the track within four weeks of his latest start his UK chase record reads: 1113641153172 (6-13), improving to: 1111312 (5-7) if we discard his runs on tracks with significant undulations (e.g. Cheltenham).

MAJAALES (USA)
5yo b g (T R George)

Race type	Non-handicap hurdles: 765 (0-3)
	Handicap hurdles: 11018 (3-5)
Conclusion:	he improved for the switch to handicap company.
Distance	2m-2m1f: 765110 (2-6)
	2m3f: 1 (1-1)
	2m4f110y: 8 (0-1)
Conclusion:	he disappointed when upped to an extended 2m4f at Uttoxeter on his final start last term but jumped poorly that day and it is too early to say that he doesn't stay the trip.
Going	Good or faster: 0 (0-1)
	Good to soft: 71118 (3-5)
	Soft/heavy: 65 (0-2)
Conclusion:	all his wins have come on good to soft going.

Summary of ideal conditions When racing in handicap hurdles his record stands at: 11018 (3-5), improving to: 111 (3-3) at 2m-2m3f on good to soft or softer going.

MAJORCA

7yo b g (Ferdy Murphy)

Race type	Hdl: 6084106486F913035 (2-17)
	Chs: 162U1643 (2-8)
Conclusion:	he's effective over hurdles and fences.
Distance	2m-2m2f: 64106486F913035162U164 (4-22)
	2m3f-2m5f: 083 (0-3)
Conclusion:	all his wins have come over trips of about 2m.
Going	Good to firm or faster: 8106F1 (2-6)
	Good: 4861303562643 (1-13)
	Good to soft: 69U1 (1-4)
	Soft/heavy: 04 (0-2)
Conclusion:	he seems best on fast ground.
Fresh (absence since last race)	
	42 days or longer: 6041401621 (3-10)
	35-41 days: 14 (1-2)
	28-34 days: no runs
	27 days or less: 80666F9335U63 (0-13)
Conclusion:	all his wins have come when rested for at least five weeks.

Summary of ideal conditions Combine a distance of 2m-2m2f with running fresh (after a break of five weeks or more) and his record since his hurdles debut becomes: 4141016214 (4-10).

MALJIMAR (IRE)

8yo b g (Nick Williams)

Race type	NHF: 2 (0-1)
	Hdl: 6P14 (1-4)
	Chs: F23132U41U (2-10)
Conclusion:	he has yet to finish out of the first four places when completing the course over fences.
Distance	2m-2m1f: 264 (0-3)
	2m2f-2m5f: P1423132U1U (3-11)
	3m+: F (0-1)
Conclusion:	he seems best at about 2m4f.
Going	Good to firm or faster: 14 (1-2)
	Good: 6P24 (0-4)
	Good to soft: 2F231U (1-6)
	Soft: 31U (1-3)
	Heavy: no runs
Conclusion:	his best recent efforts have come on good to soft or soft going.

Fresh (absence since last race)

> 42 days or longer: 26P1F12U1 (3-9)
> 28-41 days: 3U (0-2)
> 27 days or less: 4234 (0-4)

Conclusion: he runs especially well when fresh.

Summary of ideal conditions When running fresh (after a break of six weeks or longer) his record becomes: 26P1F12U1 (3-9), improving to: F12U1 (2-5) for current trainer Nick Williams. From left to right: F – tipped up four out at Chepstow when still travelling well (3m, good to soft), 1st – landed a soft-ground 2m3f handicap chase at Newbury, 2nd – beaten by a neck in a valuable 19-runner handicap chase at Cheltenham, U – unseated rider at the first fence, and 1st. He goes well at Cheltenham and is likely to make his seasonal debut in the Paddy Power Gold Cup at that venue in mid-November.

MANBOW (IRE)

10yo b g (M D Hammond)

Race type	NHF: 88 (0-2)
	Hdl: PP8 (0-3)
	Ch: 1112P122PP23F12PP (5-17)
Conclusion:	he's best over fences.
Distance	2m-2m3f: 88 (0-2)
	2m4f-2m5f110y: PP223F1P (1-8)
	2m6f-2m7f: 81 (1-2)
	3m+: 11P122P22P (3-10)
Conclusion:	he needs a trip of at least 2m4f.
Going	Good to firm or faster: 1212P (2-5)
	Good: 8P8112F (2-7)
	Good to soft: 82P12P3 (1-7)
	Soft/heavy: PPP (0-3)
Conclusion:	he has yet to win on ground slower than good to soft.
Jockey	G Lee: 8111122PPF1PP (5-13)
	Others: 8PP82P232 (0-9)
Conclusion:	all his wins came when ridden by Graham Lee.

Course (chase starts only)

Aintree: F (0-1)
Haydock: 2 (0-1)
Kelso: 1 (1-1)
Kempton: P (0-1)
Newbury: P (0-1)
Perth: P (0-1)
Sandown: 2P (0-2)
Wetherby: 1112P2312 (4-9)

Conclusion: he has a good record at Wetherby and has yet to win on a right-handed track.

Summary of ideal conditions When racing over fences on good or faster going his record is: 11122F12P (4-9), improving to: 11212 (3-5) at Wetherby only.

MASSINI SUNSET (IRE)

8yo b g (N R Mitchell)

Race type   Hdl: P585P550 (0-8)
                   Chs: P83131U51214 (4-12)

Conclusion: he improved for the switch to fences.

Going (chase starts only)

Good or faster: P8U (0-3)
Good to soft: 31514 (2-5)
Soft/heavy: 1312 (2-4)

Conclusion: the softer the going, the better he runs.

Field size (chase starts only)

15 or more runners: 311 (2-3)
12-14 runners: no runs
11 or fewer runners: P83U51214 (2-9)

Conclusion: two of his four wins came in big fields (15 and 16 ran) but he is effective in smaller line-ups when the early pace is strong.

Summary of ideal conditions When racing over fences on good to soft or softer going his record becomes: 313151214 (4-9), improving to: 311 (2-3) in fields of 15 or more runners, with the sole defeat by less than two lengths when a 100-1 shot.

MASTER SEBASTIAN
9yo ch g (Miss Lucinda V Russell)

Race type	NHF: 253 (0-3)
	Hdl: 6242145 (1-7)
	Chs: 43165PP5624411368971139 (5-23)
Conclusion:	he's best over fences.
Going	Good or faster: 26597 (0-5)
	Good to soft: P5439 (0-5)
	Soft: 3241415P241381 (4-14)
	Heavy: 524366161 (2-9)
Conclusion:	he needs soft or heavy going.
Time of year	Jan: 511111 (5-6)
	Feb: 46313 (1-5)
	Mar: 569 (0-3)
	Apr: 35P8 (0-4)
	May-Sep: P (0-1)
	Oct: 64569 (0-5)
	Nov: 224247 (0-6)
	Dec: 234 (0-3)
Conclusion:	he peaks at the same time each year, winning five of his six starts in January (his only non-January win came on 6 February).

Summary of ideal conditions When racing over hurdles or fences in January his record is: 11111 (5-5), with three of the wins coming in the same Class 3 handicap chase over 2m4f at Ayr, a race that will no doubt be his target this season.

MIGHTY MOOSE (IRE)
8yo b g (Nick Williams)

Race type	Non-handicap chases: P593 (0-4)
	Handicap chases: 1411635524P (3-11)
Conclusion:	he improved for the switch to handicap company.
Distance	2m-2m2f: no runs
	2m3f-2m5f: 11154 (3-5)
	2m5f110y-2m6f110y: 65P (0-3)
	2m7f+: P593432 (0-7)
Conclusion:	he is best at trips of about 2m4f.
Going	Good to firm or faster: no runs
	Good: 11P (2-3)
	Good to soft: P965 (0-4)
	Soft: 514354 (1-6)
	Heavy: 32 (0-2)
Conclusion:	he seems best on good or softer going.

Summary of ideal conditions When racing in handicap chases his record is: 1411635524P (3-11), improving to: 11154 (3-5) at trips of 2m3f-2m5f. His form tailed off towards the end of last season but he has since had a wind operation which, if successful, should ensure that he finds another race or two this term.

MIKO DE BEAUCHENE (FR)

8yo b g (R H & Mrs S Alner)

Race type	NHF: 49 (0-2)
	Hdl: 22224P182323522 (1-15)
	Chs: 1P2U11P (3-7)
Conclusion:	he has winning form over hurdles and fences.
Going	Good or faster: 49PP (0-4)
	Good to soft: 242512U212 (2-10)
	Soft/heavy: 22218323P1 (2-10)
Conclusion:	he needs good to soft or softer going.
Track	Left-handed: 924P1232512U2112P (4-17)
	Right-handed: 422283P (0-7)
Conclusion:	he performs best on left-handed tracks.
Fresh (absence since last race)	
	First two runs each season or after a break of six weeks +: 49181P211 (4-9)
	Other runs: 22224P232352U2P (0-15)

Summary of ideal conditions When racing left-handed on good to soft or softer going his record over obstacles stands at: 241232512U2112 (4-14), improving to: 11211 (4-5) when fresh (first two runs each season or after a break of six weeks or more).

MISSIS POTTS

7yo b m (P J Hobbs)

Race type	NHF: 4 (0-1)
	Hdl: 321P111965 (4-10)
	Chs: 1 (1-1)
Conclusion:	she has a good-strike rate over hurdles and won her sole chase start.
Distance	2m-2m1f: 41119165 (4-8)
	2m3f-2m5f: 32P1 (1-4)
Conclusion:	most of her wins have come at about 2m but she does stay further.

Going	Good to firm or faster: 9 (0-1)
	Good: 411 (2-3)
	Good to soft: P165 (1-4)
	Soft: 211 (2-3)
	Heavy: 3 (0-1)
Conclusion:	she has yet to win on extremes of going.
Field size	12 or more runners: 41P1965 (2-7)
	11 or fewer runners: 32111 (3-5)
Conclusion:	she has a good record in small fields.
Class	1: P965 (0-4)
	2: 1 (1-1)
	3: 11 (2-2)
	4: 43211 (2-5)
Conclusion:	she has yet to win in Class 1 company.

Summary of ideal conditions When racing over hurdles or fences her record is: 321P1119165 (5-11), improving to: 3211111 (5-7) in Class 2 or lower company, with the first defeat excusable as she was making her hurdling debut in stamina-sapping conditions (2m4f, heavy).

MISTER QUASIMODO
8yo b g (C L Tizzard)

Race type	NHF: 1410 (2-4)
	Hdl: 2141220F (2-8)
	Chs: P21FP2313P103 (3-13)
Conclusion:	he is effective over hurdles and fences.
Distance	2m-2m2f110y: 141022F31303 (3-12)
	2m3f-2m6f: 21101FP2P1 (4-10)
	2m7f+: 4P2 (0-3)
Conclusion:	he seems best at trips short of 2m7f.
Going	Good or faster: 00233 (0-5)
	Good to soft: 1412PF1310 (4-10)
	Soft: 14122FP (2-7)
	Heavy: 21P (1-3)
Conclusion:	he seems happiest on slow going.
Field size (chase starts only)	
	12 or more runners: 0 (0-1)
	8-11 runners: 21P33 (1-5)
	7 or fewer runners: PF213P1 (2-7)
Conclusion:	he's a front-runner and is better able to dominate when racing in small fields.

Summary of ideal conditions Throw out his runs at 2m7f or further and his record on good to soft or softer going becomes: 141211221FPF13P10 (7-17), improving to: 14121122F13P1 (6-13) if we also discard his chase runs in fields of eight or more runners.

MOKUM (FR)

7yo b g (A W Carroll)

Race type	Hdl: 862357076707P7 (0-14)
	Chs: U12F413233P3411FP2 (4-18)
Conclusion:	he's best over fences.

Going (chase runs only)

	Good or faster: 24133P341F (2-10)
	Good to soft: 112 (2-3)
	Soft: UF23P (0-5)
	Heavy: no runs
Conclusion:	he is unproven on extremes of going.
Fresh	Seasonal debuts: 87P7 (0-4)
Conclusion:	he has always needed his first run of the season.

Course (chase starts only)

	Cheltenham: 2 (0-1)
	Leicester: 4133341 (2-7)
	Newbury: P (0-1)
	Sandown: U21F (1-4)
	Stratford: F (0-1)
	Towcester: 123 (1-3)
	Wetherby: P (0-1)
Conclusion:	his best efforts, and indeed the majority of his runs, have taken place on tracks with stiff uphill finishes.

Summary of ideal conditions When racing over fences on stiff tracks (e.g. Cheltenham and Sandown), outside of his seasonal debuts, his record becomes: U124132333411F2 (4-15), improving to: 1241333411F2 (4-12) on good to soft or faster going only.

MON MOME (FR)
8yo b g (Miss Venetia Williams)

Race type	Hdl: 7U362453 (0-8)
	Chs: U2121121U422434P609 (4-19)
Conclusion:	he's best over fences.
Going	Good to firm or faster: no runs
	Good: 45U22U09 (0-8)
	Good to soft: 7214P36 (1-7)
	Soft/heavy: U36121142243 (3-12)
Conclusion:	he seems best suited by good to soft or softer going.
Fresh	Seasonal debuts: 7U4P (0-4)
Conclusion:	he has always needed his first run of the season.
Class (chase runs only)	
	1: U22434P609 (0-10)
	2: 214 (1-3)
	3: U2211 (2-5)
	4: 1 (1-1)
Conclusion:	he has yet to win in Class 1 company.

Summary of ideal conditions When racing over fences on good to soft or softer going, excluding seasonal debuts, his record is: 1211122434609 (4-13), improving to: 12111 (4-5) in Class 2 or lower company only.

MOON OVER MIAMI (GER)
7yo b g (C J Mann)

Race type	Hdl: 48112212 (3-8)
	Chs: 5141P6 (2-6)
Conclusion:	he's effective over hurdles and fences.
Going	Good or faster: 1122125 (3-7)
	Good to soft: 48P6 (0-4)
	Soft/heavy: 141 (2-3)
Conclusion:	he seems effective on any going.
Track	Left-handed: 481111P6 (4-8)
	Right-handed: 122254 (1-6)
Conclusion:	four of his five wins have come on left-handed tracks – at Cheltenham (twice), Uttoxeter and Newbury.
Fresh (absence since last race)	
	42 days or longer: 425P (0-4)
	29-41 days: 26 (0-2)
	28 days or less: 81121141 (5-8)
Conclusion:	all his wins came when returned to the track 28 days or less after his previous outing.

Summary of ideal conditions When racing left-handed after a recent run (28 days or less) his record becomes: 81111 (4-5), with the sole defeat coming in a Grade 2 contest on only his second start over jumps for which he started at 66-1.

MOSSBANK (IRE)
8yo b g (Michael Hourigan)

Race type	NHF: 7 (0-1)
	Hdl: 11235F5 (2-7)
	Chs: 125F0P11223 (3-11)
Conclusion:	he is effective over hurdles and fences.
Fresh	First two runs each season: 7111211 (5-7)
	Third or subsequent runs: 235F55F0P223 (0-12)
Conclusion:	he has yet to win outside of his first two starts of the season. He has also performed well after a mid-season layoff, finishing runner-up in the Ryanair Chase at the 2008 Cheltenham Festival after a break of 11 weeks.

Summary of ideal conditions Combine hurdle or chase starts with running first or second-time out and his record becomes: 111211 (5-6), with the sole defeat by a short head. These wins came at 2m2f-3m on ground ranging from good through to soft.

MOTORWAY (IRE)
7yo b g (P J Hobbs)

Race type	Hdl: 3111F1050810 (5-12)
Conclusion:	he has a good strike-rate over hurdles.
Distance	2m-2m2f: 3111F1010 (5-9)
	2m3f-2m5f: 058 (0-3)
Conclusion:	he's best at about 2m.
Going	Good to firm: 5 (0-1)
	Good: 111080 (3-6)
	Good to soft: 31F0 (1-4)
	Soft: 1 (1-1)
	Heavy: no runs
Field size	12 or more runners: 305080 (0-6)
	11 or fewer runners: 111F11 (5-6)
Conclusion:	he has often struggled in big fields.

Summary of ideal conditions When racing in fields of 11 or fewer runners his record reads: 111F11 (5-6).

MOUS OF MEN (FR)

5yo b g (D E Pipe)

Race type	Non-handicap hurdles: 550 (0-3)
	Handicap hurdles: 24211801 (3-8)
Conclusion:	he improved for the switch to handicap hurdle company and is expected to make the grade over fences this term.
Distance	2m-2m1f110y: 550180 (1-6)
	2m2f-2m3f: 242 (0-3)
	2m4f: 11 (2-2)
Conclusion:	he improved for the step up to 2m4f last season, winning big-field handicap hurdles at Doncaster and Sandown.
Going	Good to firm: 4 (0-1)
	Good: 5221801 (2-7)
	Good to soft: no runs
	Soft: 501 (1-3)
	Heavy: no runs
Conclusion:	he seems to handle most ground conditions.
Track	Left-handed: 22180 (1-5)
	Right-handed: 550411 (2-6)
Conclusion:	he has winning form on both left-handed and right-handed tracks.
Field size	12 or more runners: 50221101 (3-8)
	11 or fewer runners: 548 (0-3)
Conclusion:	he seems best coming late off a strong pace and it's probably no coincidence that his wins came in big fields (14, 20 and 17 ran).
Fresh (absence since last race)	
	42 days or longer: 5428 (0-4)
	28-41 days: 20 (0-2)
	27 days or less: 50111 (3-5)
Conclusion:	all his wins have come after a recent outing (24, 21 and eight days).

Summary of ideal conditions Since qualified to race in handicaps his record reads: 24211801 (3-8), improving to: 22111 (3-5) when racing at 2m2f or further (or at shorter trips on soft going).

MR POINTMENT (IRE)
9yo b g (P F Nicholls)

Race type	NHF: 14 (1-2)
	Hdl: 1415 (2-4)
	Chs: 122416P (2-7)
Conclusion:	he is effective over hurdles and fences.
Going	Good to firm or faster: no runs
	Good: 1546P (1-5)
	Good to soft: 41411 (3-5)
	Soft: 122 (1-3)
	Heavy: no runs
Conclusion:	he won a good-ground bumper back in December 2004 but his subsequent wins have come on good to soft or softer going.

Fresh (absence since last race)

	35 days or longer: 141112416P (5-10)
	34 days or less: 452 (0-3)
Conclusion:	he's best when fresh.
Track	Left-handed: 14415122416P (4-12)
	Right-handed: 1 (1-1)
Conclusion:	he won his sole right-handed start (over hurdles at Market Rasen) but has tended to jump out to his left since switched to fences and is likely to prove best left-handed.

Summary of ideal conditions When running fresh (after a break of five weeks or longer) his record is: 141112416P (5-10), improving to: 11121 (4-5) on good to soft or softer going, with the sole defeat by Denman.

MY IMMORTAL
6yo b g (D E Pipe)

Race type	Hdl: 262263104013 (2-12)
	Chs: 112F3U00 (2-8)
Conclusion:	he has winning form over hurdles and fences.
Distance	2m-2m2f: 2622610 (1-7)
	2m3f-2m7f: 3403 (0-4)
	3m+: 1112F3U00 (3-9)
Conclusion:	he improved for the step up to 3m+.
Going	Good to firm or faster: 23111 (3-5)
	Good: 221320 (1-6)
	Good to soft: 6640U (0-5)
	Soft/heavy: 0F30 (0-4)
Conclusion:	he prefers good or faster going.

Field size (chase runs only)

> 12 or more runners: U00 (0-3)
>
> 8-11 runners: 2F3 (0-3)
>
> 7 or fewer runners: 11 (2-2)

Conclusion: his jumping remains far from perfect and he is likely to prove best in small fields.

Summary of ideal conditions When racing on good or faster going his record reads: 22231131120 (4-11), with the 'duck egg' coming in a 19-runner Grade 3 handicap chase.

NATAL (FR)

7yo b g (P F Nicholls)

Distance   2m-2m2f: 115114361232 (5-12)

> 2m3f-2m5f110y: 1141221F (4-8)
>
> 3m+: 7U48 (0-4)

Conclusion: he seems best at trips short of 3m.

Track   Flat: 11113111221F2 (8-13)

> Significant undulations: 5461247U483 (1-11)

Conclusion: he prefers flat tracks.

Summary of ideal conditions If we discard his runs on tracks with significant undulations (e.g. Chepstow and Cheltenham) his record becomes: 11113111221F2 (8-13), with all these runs taking place at 2m-2m5f110y.

NENUPHAR COLLONGES (FR)

7yo b g (A King)

Race type   Hdl: F212140 (2-7)

> Chs: 6111F21 (4-7)

Conclusion: a winner over fences in France, he began his UK career with handicap chase wins at Bangor and Hereford but was campaigned exclusively over hurdles last season, landing a Grade 1 contest at the Cheltenham Festival.

Distance (UK runs only)

> 2m-2m7f110y: 11F222 (2-6)
>
> 3m+: 1114 (3-4)

Conclusion: he improved for the step up to 3m+.

Going (UK runs only)

> Good to firm or faster: no runs
> Good: 14 (1-2)
> Good to soft: 1F1 (2-3)
> Soft: 1212 (2-4)
> Heavy: 2 (0-1)

Conclusion: he seems best on good to soft or softer going.

Track (UK runs only)

> Aintree: 4 (0-1)
> Bangor: 1 (1-1)
> Cheltenham: 211 (2-3)
> Exeter: F (0-1)
> Hereford: 1 (1-1)
> Leicester: 2 (0-1)
> Uttoxeter: 1 (1-1)
> Warwick: 2 (0-1)

Conclusion: he takes an age to hit top gear in his races and is clearly happiest on stiff/galloping tracks such as Cheltenham.

Summary of ideal conditons Since joining his current trainer Alan King his record reads: 11F2121214 (5-10), improving to: 1114 (3-4) at 3m or further, with the sole defeat excusable as he found the combination of Aintree's sharp Mildmay course and good ground an insufficient test of stamina.

NEPTUNE COLLONGES (FR)

7yo gr g (P F Nicholls)

Race type   Hdl: 14121136 (4-8)
    Ch: 1111U121F813131 (9-15)

Conclusion: he's effective over hurdles and fences.

Going   Good or faster: 1 (1-1)
    Good to yielding: 1 (1-1)
    Good to soft: 423168313 (2-9)
    Soft/heavy: 1111U111112F (9-12)

Conclusion: he has a fine record on soft or heavy going but coped with fast conditions when landing a Grade 1 contest at Punchestown in April 2007.

Field size   12 or more runners: 1483 (1-4)
    8-11 runners: 11U123216F131 (6-13)
    7 or fewer runners: 111111 (6-6)

Conclusion: he still takes the occasional liberty with his fences and is likely to prove best in small fields.

Summary of ideal conditions When racing in small fields (11 or fewer runners) his record is: 111U1112113216F12311 (12-20), including a six-from-six haul in fields of seven or fewer runners.

NEVERTIKA (FR)

7yo b g (Mrs K Walton)

Race type	NHF: 5422 (0-4)
	Fixed brush hurdles: 1323 (1-4)
	Standard hurdles: 34 (0-2)
	Chs: 111FF (3-5)
Conclusion:	he is unbeaten when completing the course over fences.
Distance	2m-2m2f: 542241F (1-7)
	2m3f-2m5f: 1323311F (3-8)
Conclusion:	his sole 2m win came on a very stiff track (Hexham) and he is likely to prove best at 2m4f or further.
Going	Good to firm: no runs
	Good: 5131 (2-4)
	Good to soft: 43FF (0-4)
	Soft: 22311 (2-5)
	Heavy: 24 (0-2)
Conclusion:	he is effective on good or softer going.

Summary of ideal When racing over fences or fixed brush hurdles his record reads: 1323111FF (4-9), improving to: 111F (3-4) in chases of 2m3f or further (or over shorter trips on soft/heavy going).

NOTANOTHERDONKEY (IRE)

8yo b g (M J Scudamore)

Race type	NHF: 0833 (0-4)
	Hdl: 065P376 (0-7)
	Chs: 23731235721FPP (2-14)
Conclusion:	he's best over fences.
Fresh	First two runs each season: 0830321221 (2-10)
	Third or subsequent runs: 365P37673357FPP (0-15)
Conclusion:	both his wins came early in the season (October and November).

Summary of ideal conditions Combine chase starts with racing first or second-time out and his record becomes: 21221 (2-5). From left to right: 2nd – stayed on well over an extended 2m4f at Cheltenham (20-1), 1st – scored by nine lengths in a 15-runner handicap at Cheltenham (13-2), 2nd – struggled to see out a stiff 3m at Exeter (100-30), 2nd – beaten by a length over 3m at Exeter, again not quite lasting home (5-1), and 1st – justified ' 5-8 favouritism by two lengths on fast ground at Wetherby (3m1f). He's happiest on good or faster going and seems ideally served by a trip of about 2m5f-2m6f, though he does stay further when conditions are not testing.

NUDGE AND NURDLE (IRE)

7yo b g (N A Twiston-Davies)

Race type	Hdl: 43S28813261 (2-11)
	Chs: 1540F1 (2-6)
Conclusion:	he has winning form over hurdles and fences.
Distance	2m-2m3f: 43 (0-2)
	2m4f-2m6f110y: S281211540 (3-10)
	3m+: 836F1 (1-5)
Conclusion:	he has winning form from 2m4f-3m.
Track	Left-handed: 43S8361540F (1-11)
	Right-handed: 281211 (3-6)
Conclusion:	he scraped home by a head at left-handed Kelso on his chase debut but often earns the comment 'jumped right' and will prove best when racing right-handed.

Summary of ideal conditions When racing right-handed his record reads: 281211 (3-6).

OAKFIELD LEGEND
7yo b g (P S Payne)

Race type	NHF: 50 (0-2)
	Hdl: P67P45 (0-6)
	Chs: 1P6472F12F3232 (2-14)
Conclusion:	he's best over fences.
Distance	2m-2m6f: 50PP4P47353 (0-11)
	3m+: 67162F12F22 (2-11)
Conclusion:	he needs a trip of at least 3m.
Going	Good to firm or faster: 57P15 (1-5)
	Good: P6P41647F332 (1-12)
	Good to soft: 2F2 (0-3)
	Soft/heavy: 2 (0-1)
	Polytrack: 0 (0-1)
Conclusion:	he's best on good or faster going.

Summary of ideal Combine chase starts with racing over 3m or further, on good or faster going, and his record becomes: 161F2 (2-5). From left to right: 1st – made a winning chase debut at Worcester (33-1), 6th – only beaten by around six lengths at Worcester despite a bad blunder (16-1), 1st – scored by nine lengths at Taunton (20-1), F – 12 lengths clear and looked certain to win before falling two out at Sandown (2-1), and 2nd – 33 lengths clear of the third placed horse when just over two lengths behind Hermano Cordobes at Newton Abbot (6-1).

OLD BENNY
7yo b g (A King)

Race type	NHF: 227 (0-3)
	Hdl: 5221127 (2-7)
	Chs: 32214 (1-5)
Conclusion:	he's effective over hurdles and fences.
Distance	1m5f-2m7f: 4275 (0-4)
	3m+: 22112732214 (3-11)
Conclusion:	he needs a trip of at least 3m and he stays marathon distances well – his latest win came in the 4m National Hunt Chase Challenge Cup at the Cheltenham Festival.
Going	Good or faster: 4224 (0-4)
	Good to soft: 5721 (1-4)
	Soft/heavy: 2721132 (2-7)
Conclusion:	he's effective on good ground but all his wins have come on good to soft or softer going.

Summary of ideal conditions When racing at 3m or further his record is: 22112732214 (3-11), with the sole unplaced effort coming in a Pertemps qualifier (the fourth place came in a 24-runner handicap chase). On good to soft or softer going only his record at 3m or further improves to: 21173221 (3-8).

OLLIE MAGERN

10yo b g (N A Twiston-Davies)

Race type	NHF: 00 (0-2)
	Hdl: 02421121110564 (5-14)
	Ch: 111421U12176405U4716447 (7-23)
Conclusion:	he's effective over hurdles and fences.
Track	Left-handed: 022121105611142U121705416447 (9-28)
	Right-handed: 004114164U7 (3-11)
Conclusion:	he has sometimes displayed a tendency to jump out to his left on right-handed tracks and will prove best when racing on left-handed circuits.
Field size	12 or more runners: 00024054207 (0-11)
	10-11 runners: 26U4 (0-4)
	8-9 runners: 1211657 (3-7)
	7 or fewer runners: 11114111U12743164 (9-17)
Conclusion:	all his wins have come in single-figure fields.
Class	Grade 1: 12760476 (1-8)
	Grade 2: U114514 (3-7)
	Grade 3: 04247 (0-5)
	Others: 0002421121115641110 (8-19)
Conclusion:	he scored in Grade 1 company as a novice but tends to struggle at that level these days.

Summary of ideal conditions Combine hurdle or chase starts with racing in small fields (nine or fewer runners) and his record becomes: 11211141111U121764 547164 (12-24), improving to: 1211111U11514 (9-13) on left-handed tracks and in Grade 2 or lower company. He has won on soft ground but seems best on a fast surface.

O'MALEY (FR)
6yo b g (P F Nicholls)

Race type	Hdl: 6 (0-1)
	Chs: 34F11241 (3-8)
Conclusion:	he's best over fences.
Distance	2m-2m5f: 364 (0-3)
	2m6f+: F11241 (3-6)
Conclusion:	he needs a trip of at least 2m6f.
Going	Good or faster: 1141 (3-4)
	Good to soft: 34 (0-2)
	Soft/heavy: 6F2 (0-3)
Conclusion:	he's best on good or faster going.
Course	Bangor: 4 (0-1)
	Fontwell: 1124 (2-4)
	Kempton: 6 (0-1)
	Newbury: 3F (0-2)
	Newton Abbot: 1 (1-1)
Conclusion:	his wins have come on sharp tracks.
Headgear	Blinkers: 4 (0-1)
Conclusion:	he jumped poorly when tried in blinkers — finishing a 21-length last of four in a novice chase at Fontwell.

Summary of ideal conditions When racing on good or faster going, without headgear, his record becomes: 111 (3-3).

OPENIDE
7yo b g (B W Duke)

Race type	NHF: 1 (1-1)
	Hdl: 8716P230422060120650 (2-20)
	Chs: 1122P0P503P28 (2-13)
Conclusion:	he is effective over hurdles and fences.
Going	Good to firm or faster: P310 (1-4)
	Good: 112000122P50380 (3-15)
	Good to soft: 874220652 (0-9)
	Yielding to soft: 1 (1-1)
	Soft/heavy: 626PP (0-5)
Conclusion:	all his wins have come on ground faster than soft.
Field size	12 or more runners: 187P2020020P5003P28 (1-19)
	10-11 runners: 50 (0-2)
	9 or fewer runners: 16342611122P6 (4-13)
Conclusion:	since winning a 13-runner bumper on his debut, all his wins have come in single-figure fields.

Summary of ideal conditions When racing in bumpers, or in small fields (nine or fewer runners) over jumps, his record on ground faster than soft stands at: 1134111226 (5-10).

OPERA MUNDI (FR)
6yo b g (P F Nicholls)

Race type	Hdl: 21U (1-3)
	Chs: 11201PP (3-7)
Conclusion:	he has winning form over hurdles and fences.
Distance	2m-2m110y: 2U2 (0-3)
	2m1f-2m5f: 1110 (3-4)
	3m-3m1f: 1P (1-2)
	4m+: P (0-1)
Conclusion:	his latest win came at 3m but he is effective over shorter trips.
Going	Good or faster: 2PP (0-3)
	Good to soft: U0 (0-2)
	Soft/heavy: 11121 (4-5)
Conclusion:	he prefers soft or heavy going.

Summary of ideal conditions Combine hurdle or chase starts with running on soft or heavy going and his record becomes: 11121 (4-5), improving to: 1111 (4-4) at 2m1f or further.

PABLO DU CHARMIL (FR)
7yo ch g (D E Pipe)

Race type	Hdl: 22U00 (0-5)
	Chs: 111016358 (4-9)
Conclusion:	he won over hurdles in France but his UK wins have come over fences.
Going	Good to firm or faster: 1 (1-1)
	Good: 01638 (1-5)
	Good to soft: 2U1050 (1-6)
	Soft: no runs
	Heavy: 21 (1-2)
Conclusion:	he seems effective on any going.
Field size	12 or more runners: 2U000 (0-5)
	10-11 runner: 638 (0-3)
	8-9 runner: no runs
	6-7 runners: 25 (0-2)
	5 or fewer runners: 1111 (4-4)
Conclusion:	his jumping remains far from fluent and all his wins have come in very small fields.

Summary of ideal conditions When racing over fences in fields of 11 or fewer runners his record becomes: 11116358 (4-8), improving to: 1111 (4-4) in fields of five or less.

PAN THE MAN (IRE)
7yo b g (J W Mullins)

Race type	NHF: 1 (1-1)
	Hdl: 29PP707 (0-7)
	Chs: 3F5P3211P6574P15228 (3-19)
Conclusion:	he's best over fences.
Distance	2m-2m2f: 15 (1-2)
	2m3f-2m4f110y: P3732117P7122 (3-13)
	2m5f-2m6f110y: 29PF5P6458 (0-10)
	3m+: P0 (0-2)
Conclusion:	his best efforts have come over trips short of 2m5f.
Going	Good to firm or faster: 135P15741 (3-9)
	Good: PF721PP75228 (1-12)
	Good to soft: 2 (0-1)
	Soft/heavy: 9P036 (0-5)
Conclusion:	he's best on fast ground.
Course	Plumpton: 2932117P1 (3-9)
Conclusion:	he won an Exeter bumper on his racecourse debut but all his subsequent wins have come at Plumpton.
Time of year	Jan-Feb: 9P (0-2)
	Mar-May: 1P3F3211P715 (4-12)
	Jun-Aug: 5P65228 (0-7)
	Sep-Oct: 74 (0-2)
	Nov-Dec: 270P (0-4)
Conclusion:	all his wins have come in the spring.
Field size (chase runs only)	
	12 or more runners: PP58 (0-4)
	8-11 runners: 3F536572 (0-8)
	7 or fewer runners: 2114P12 (3-7)
Conclusion:	all his chase wins have come in small fields.

Summary of ideal conditions When racing at trips short of 2m5f on good or faster going his record becomes: 13721157P7122 (4-13), improving to: 21112 (3-5) if we confine these efforts to the ones over fences in fields of seven or fewer runners from March to August, with the latest defeat by a nose.

PARSONS LEGACY (IRE)
10yo b g (P J Hobbs)

Race type	NHF: 048 (0-3)
	Hdl: 3221P104P2 (2-10)
	Chs: 13216357P2921542354 (3-19)
Conclusion:	he's effective over hurdles and fences.
Distance	2m-2m2f110y: 04833 (0-5)
	2m3f-2m5f110y: 21P1013 (3-7)
	2m6f-2m7f110y: 4217 (1-4)
	3m+: P2635P2921542354 (1-16)
Conclusion:	his latest win came over an extended 3m1f and he went close in the 2007 Scottish Grand National.
Going	Good to firm or faster: 1223 (1-4)
	Good: 4313579215 (2-10)
	Good to soft: 31P126P24 (2-9)
	Soft/heavy: 04832P054 (0-9)
Conclusion:	he is effective when there's a little cut in the ground but seems best on good or faster going.
Field size	12 or more runners: 04833P04P6359215235 (1-19)
	10-11 runners: 227P2 (0-5)
	9 or fewer runners: 11132144 (4-8)
Conclusion:	he tends to make jumping errors when running in big fields.
Fresh (absence since last race)	
	35 days or longer: 010167P2214235 (3-14)
	34 days or less: 48332P14P232135954 (2-18)
Conclusion:	he seems best when fresh.

Summary of ideal conditions When running fresh (after a break of five weeks or longer) his record over hurdles or fences on good to soft or faster going becomes: 1167P221235 (3-11).

PETITE MARGOT
9yo b m (N A Twiston-Davies)

Race type	NHF: 9431 (1-4)
	Hdl: 11142341P15309077 (5-17)
	Ch: 1126PP54122212P (4-15)
Conclusion:	she's effective over hurdles and fences.
Distance	2m-2m2f110y: 9431 (1-4)
	2m3f-2m5f110y: 14312 (2-5)
	2m6f+: 114231P15090716PP541227212P (7-27)
Conclusion:	she seems to need at least 2m6f these days (her last two wins have come at 3m4f).

Field size	12 or more runners: 9434234P5090P522P (0-17)
	8-11 runners: 11376P127 (3-9)
	7 or fewer runners: 1111112421 (7-10)
Conclusion:	she tends to lose her position in big fields and has lost all her starts in fields of 12 or more runners.

Summary of ideal conditions When racing in small fields (11 or fewer runners over hurdles, seven or fewer over fences) her record is: 111111371124721 (9-15).

POLITICAL PADDY

6yo b g (R Nixon)

Race type	NHF: 86 (0-2)
	Hdl: 763U24 (0-6)
Conclusion:	he has yet to win over hurdles but has shown promise on more than one occasion.
Distance	2m-2m2f: 86 (0-2)
	2m3f-2m5f: 34 (0-2)
	2m6f-2m7f: U2 (0-2)
	3m+: 76 (0-2)
Conclusion:	he went close over 2m6f110y at Kelso last term and might stay further.
Going	Good to firm: 3 (0-1)
	Good: 864 (0-3)
	Good to soft: no runs
	Soft: 7U (0-2)
	Heavy: 62 (0-2)
Conclusion:	his best effort came on heavy going but he has placed form on fast ground.
Headgear	Cheekpieces: 324 (0-3)
	Without headgear: 8676U (0-5)
Conclusion:	his best efforts have come when wearing cheekpieces.

Summary of ideal conditions When racing over hurdles in cheekpieces his record is: 324 (0-3). From left-to-right: 3rd – placed at 100-1 on fast ground at Newcastle (2m4f), 2nd – beaten by a nose on heavy going over the extended 2m6f trip at Kelso (11-1) and 4th – seemed to find 2m4f on good ground an insufficient test of stamina at Perth (7-2). His half-brothers Political Sox and Political Cruise both won several races and it's surely only a matter of time before he gets off the mark.

PUNJABI

5yo b g (N J Henderson)

Race type	Hdl: 114214231 (4-9)
Conclusion:	he has yet to finish out of the frame when racing over hurdles.
Distance	2m-2m1f: 114214231 (4-9)
Conclusion:	all his hurdles runs have taken place at about 2m.
Going	Good or faster: 1211 (3-4)
	Good to soft: 4423 (0-4)
	Soft/heavy: 1 (1-1)
Conclusion:	he handles slow going but seems best on good or faster ground.
Fresh	Seasonal debuts: 14 (1-2)
Conclusion:	he won first-time out during the 2006/2007 season but ran as though needing his reappearance run last term.

Summary of ideal conditions When racing over hurdles his record is: 114214231 (4-9), improving to: 1211 (3-4) on good or faster going, with the sole defeat by subsequent Champion Hurdle winner Katchit.

PUR DE SIVOLA (FR)

5yo b g (A King)

Race type	Hdl: 31P (1-3)
	Chs: 2121F4 (2-6)
Conclusion:	he's effective over hurdles and fences.
Track	Left-handed: 3P2 (0-3)
	Right-handed: 1121F4 (3-6)
Conclusion:	he jumped out to his right when runner-up at left-handed Warwick in November 2007 and is likely to prove best on right-handed tracks.
Going	Good or faster: 2F (0-2)
	Good to soft: 3P1214 (2-6)
	Soft/heavy: 1 (1-1)
Conclusion:	all his wins have come on good to soft or softer going.

Summary of ideal conditions When racing right-handed his record is: 1121F4 (3-6), with the latest defeat excusable as he finished lame. He has winning form from 2m-2m5f and is unbeaten in two starts at Wincanton.

RACING DEMON (IRE)
6yo b g (Miss H C Knight)

Race type	NHF: 1 (1-1)
	Hdl: 21312F (2-6)
	Ch: 1117U135414360 (5-14)
Conclusion:	he's effective over hurdles and fences.
Distance	2m-2m2f110y: 1213117U (4-8)
	2m3f-2m5f110y: 1211F5136 (4-9)
	3m-3m1f: 344 (0-3)
	3m4f+: 0 (0-1)
Conclusion:	he seems best at trips short of 3m.
Track	Left-handed: 2756 (0-4)
	Right-handed: 12131111U13F41430 (8-17)
Conclusion:	he has yet to win on a left-handed track.

Summary of ideal conditions Combine chase starts with racing on right-handed tracks, at trips below 3m, and his record becomes: 111U113 (5-7).

RASH MOMENT (FR)
9yo b g (Mrs K Waldron)

Race type	Hdl: 7202103P (1-8)
	Ch: P536P44P555214141F53P51UP7626P4RP41 (5-35)
Conclusion:	he's best over fences.
Distance	2m-2m2f110y: 03455 (0-5)
	2m3f-2m7f: 722103PP6P421141351U26P4RP41 (6-28)
	3m+: 5P54F5PP76 (0-10)
Conclusion:	he seems best at trips short of 3m.
Going	Good to firm or faster: 13P5PP51414F53PP76P (3-19)
	Good: 7006452151U2P4R4 (2-16)
	Good to soft: 22P46 (0-5)
	Soft/heavy: 351 (1-3)
Conclusion:	the majority of his wins have come on fast ground but he does handle slower going.

Fresh (absence since last race – chase starts only)

	42 days or longer: 3453524P (0-8)
	21-41 days: PP5P6PR4 (0-8)
	20 days or less: P56455214141FP1U761 (5-19)
Conclusion:	all his chase wins have come after a recent outing.

Race conditions (chase starts only)

> Non-handicaps: P53P43 (0-6)
>
> Handicaps: 64P555214141F5P51UP7626P4RP41 (5-29)

Conclusion: all his chase wins have taken place in handicap company.

Summary of ideal conditions Combine handicap chase starts with racing at 2m3f-2m7f, on good or faster going, when returned to the track within three weeks of his previous outing, and his record becomes: 211411U (4-7).

REGAL HEIGHTS (IRE)

7yo b g (D McCain Jnr)

Race type	NHF: 31 (1-2)
	Hdl: 45113372 (2-8)
	Chs: 352121147126P (4-12)
Conclusion:	he is effective over hurdles and fences.
Distance	2m-2m2f: 31113335111 (6-11)
	2m3f-2m6f: 4572247216P (1-11)
	3m+: 2 (0-1)
Conclusion:	all his wins have come at about 2m but he does stay further.
Going	Good or faster: 747 (0-3)
	Good to soft: 3126P (1-5)
	Soft: 4513335121 (3-10)
	Heavy: 12211 (3-5)
Conclusion:	he has yet to prove effective on good or faster going.

Fresh (absence since last race)

	42 days or longer: 34537 (0-5)
	28-41 days: 21421 (2-5)
	27 days or less: 111337512126P (5-13)
Conclusion:	he is likely to need his first run of the season.
Class	1: 3724726P (0-8)
	2: 1121 (3-4)
	3: 45 (0-2)
	4 or lower: 311133521 (4-9)
Conclusion:	he has yet to win a Class 1 event.

Summary of ideal conditions When racing on good to soft or softer going after a relatively recent run (within six weeks) his record becomes: 111335212112126P (7-16), improving to: 11135211121 (7-11) if we discard his runs in Class 1 company.

RIMSKY (IRE)
7yo gr g (N A Twiston-Davies)

Race type	NHF: 218 (1-3)
	Hdl: 11064266257 (2-11)
	Chs: 2516304 (1-7)
Conclusion:	he's effective over hurdles and fences.
Distance	2m-2m2f: 21810 (2-5)
	2m3f-2m5f: 16 (1-2)
	2m6f-3m2f: 642625251647 (1-12)
	4m+: 30 (0-2)
Conclusion:	his latest win came at 2m6f but he has placed over 4m.
Course	Aintree: 86 (0-2)
	Bangor: 1 (1-1)
	Cheltenham: 066207 (0-6)
	Chepstow: 112 (2-3)
	Exeter: 5 (0-1)
	Huntingdon: 4 (0-1)
	Leicester: 6 (0-1)
	Newbury: 24 (0-2)
	Newcastle: 3 (0-1)
	Perth: 5 (0-1)
	Towcester: 1 (1-1)
	Wetherby: 2 (0-1)
Conclusion:	he seems best on undulating tracks, his jumps wins having come at Chepstow (2) and Towcester.
Headgear	Blinkers: 642662557 (0-9)
	Without headgear: 218110216304 (4-12)
Conclusion:	he has yet to win when wearing headgear.
Fresh	First two runs or after a break of approx 5 weeks: 2111262513 (4-10)
	Other runs: 80646256047 (0-11)
Conclusion:	he runs well when fresh.

Summary of ideal conditions When running fresh (first two runs each season or after a break of about five weeks or more) his record reads: 2111262513 (4-10), improving to: 2111213 (4-7) when not wearing blinkers.

RING THE BOSS (IRE)
7yo b g (P J Hobbs)

Race type	NHF: 6R0 (0-3)
	Hdl: 4544811111632 (5-13)
	Chs: 28 (0-2)
Conclusion:	he has a good strike-rate over hurdles and made a promising start to his chase career – finishing second by a neck in a Grade 2 contest at Warwick.
Distance	2m-2m2f: 6R04111628 (3-10)
	2m3f-2m5f: 4581132 (2-7)
	2m6f+: 4 (0-1)
Conclusion:	he is effective at 2m when ground conditions are testing but is likely to prove best over longer trips.
Going	Good to firm or faster: no runs
	Good: 645163 (1-6)
	Good to yielding: 2 (0-1)
	Good to soft: R04828 (0-6)
	Soft: 411 (2-3)
	Heavy: 11 (2-2)
Conclusion:	he runs especially well on soft or heavy going.
Trainer	K G Reveley: 6R045448 (0-8)
	G A Swinbank: 111 (3-3)
	P J Hobbs: 1162832 (2-7)
Conclusion:	he was unbeaten in three outings for Alan Swinbank and has done well for Philip Hobbs.

Summary of ideal conditions Since leaving the Keith Reveley yard his record is: 1111162832 (5-10), improving to: 1111132 (5-7) at 2m3f or further (or at shorter trips on soft/heavy going), with the latest defeat by a neck in a 25-runner handicap hurdle worth £100,000 to the winner.

ROLL ALONG (IRE)
8yo b g (Carl Llewellyn)

Race type	NHF: 111 (3-3)
	Hdl: 1130 (2-4)
	Chs: 1225 (1-4)
Conclusion:	he's effective over hurdles and fences.
Fresh	First two runs each season: 111112 (5-6)
	Other runs: 13025 (1-5)
Conclusion:	he runs especially well when fresh.

Summary of ideal conditions When running on one of his first two starts each season his record reads: 111112 (5-6), with the sole defeat by a short head. He finished a 20-1 runner-up in the 2008 Royal & SunAlliance Chase on his return from a six-week layoff and can also be considered after a mid-season break. Good to soft or softer going suits him best.

ROMAN ARK

10yo gr g (J M Jefferson)

Race type	NHF: 1 (1-1)
	Hdl: 32211190 (3-8)
	Chs: U213B4P2531140810220 (4-20)
Conclusion:	he's effective over hurdles and fences.
Distance	2m-2m4f: 1221119U213B2311812 (8-19)
	2m4f110y+: 304P540020 (0-10)
Conclusion:	2m4f would appear to be the upper limit of his stamina.
Going	Good to firm or faster: no runs
	Good: 304P280 (0-7)
	Good to soft: 29U330220 (0-9)
	Soft: 21511 (3-5)
	Heavy: 11112B14 (5-8)
Conclusion:	the softer the going, the better he runs.

Summary of ideal conditions When racing on soft or heavy going his record is: 1211121B51141 (8-13), improving to: 1211121B111 (8-11) if we discard his runs beyond 2m4f.

ROOKERY LAD

10yo b g (C N Kellett)

Race type	NHF: 0 (0-1)
	Hdl: 9608492122324P01417P50 (3-22)
	Ch: 2233P25F412342472111187F705623 (5-30)
Conclusion:	he's effective over hurdles and fences.
Time of year	Mar: 49P047 (0-6)
	Apr-May: 2121412111 (6-10)
	Jun: 27105 (1-5)
	Jul: 0322862 (0-7)
	Aug: 964253 (0-6)
	Sep: 03P (0-3)
	Oct: 83P25 (0-5)
	Nov-Feb: F4123427F70 (1-11)
Conclusion:	the majority of his wins have come during April, May and June.

Track (chase starts only)

Left-handed: 23P51342471111F7623 (5-19)

Right-handed: 232F4228705 (0-11)

Conclusion: he has yet to win over fences on a right-handed track.

Summary of ideal conditions Combine left-handed chase starts with running during the period of April to July and his record becomes: 2111162 (4-7). All his wins have come over distances of 2m-2m5f, the majority on good or faster going.

RUDIVALE (IRE)

6yo ch g (C L Tizzard)

Race type   NHF: 55 (0-2)

Hdl: 4892P4332 (0-9)

Conclusion: he has yet to win a race but has placed on his last three starts.

Distance   2m-2m2f: 5589 (0-4)

2m3f-2m4f: 4 (0-1)

2m5f-2m6f: 24332 (0-5)

2m6f110y+: P (0-1)

Conclusion: his best efforts have come at 2m6f.

Going   Good to firm or faster: no runs

Good: 593 (0-3)

Good to soft: 2432 (0-4)

Soft/heavy: 548P (0-4)

Conclusion: his best efforts have come on good to soft or faster going.

Summary of ideal conditions Combine a distance of 2m3f or further with running on good to soft or faster going and his record becomes: 24332 (0-5). The lack of winning form is obviously a concern but he has often ruined his chance by pulling too hard and should find a race or two this term if he learns to settle better.

SAUNDERS ROAD (IRE)

7yo b g (P J Hobbs)

Race type   NHF: P (0-1)

Hdl: 088F114 (2-7)

Chs: 81621 (2-5)

Conclusion: he is effective over hurdles and fences.

Distance   2m-2m2f: P088F18 (1-7)

2m3f-2m5f: 1121 (3-4)

2m6f+: 46 (0-2)

Conclusion: he's best at about 2m4f.

Summary of ideal conditions When racing at 2m3f-2m5f his record reads: 1121 (3-4), with the sole defeat excusable as his stable was badly out of form at the time. All these runs took place on good or good to soft going.

SCARLET MIX (FR)

7yo gr g (Mrs A M Thorpe)

Race type	Hdl: 17820P4321192158 (4-16)
	Chs: 6PF (0-3)
Conclusion:	all his wins have taken place over hurdles.
Course	Warwick: 1111 (4-4)
	Others: 7820P43629258PF (0-15)
Conclusion:	he's a Warwick course expert.

Summary of ideal conditions Quite simply, he's a Warwick course expert, his record there being: 1111 (4-4), with all four wins coming over hurdles at 2m-2m5f and on ground ranging from good through to soft.

SERHAAPHIM

4yo gr f (N B King)

Race type	Hdl: 12261364 (2-8)
Conclusion:	all her jumps runs have taken place over hurdles.
Distance	2m-2m2f: 122614 (2-6)
	2m3f-2m5f: 36 (0-2)
Conclusion:	both her wins came at 2m.
Going	Good to firm or faster: no runs
	Good: 63 (0-2)
	Good to soft: 14 (1-2)
	Soft/heavy: 2216 (1-4)
Conclusion:	she's best on good to soft or softer going.
Course	Others: 226364 (0-6)
	Plumpton: 11 (2-2)
Conclusion:	she is unbeaten at Plumpton.

Summary of ideal conditions Combine a distance of 2m-2m2f with good to soft or softer going and her record becomes: 12214 (2-5), improving to: 11 (2-2) at Plumpton only.

SILVER INNGOT (IRE)
9yo gr g (R H & Mrs S Alner)
Race type   Hdl: 5078715 (1-7)
                   Chs: 431421197434 (3-12)
Conclusion: he's best over fences.
Fresh (absence since last race)
                   42 days or longer: 58111 (3-5)
                   28-41 days: 712974 (1-6)
                   21-27 days: 0434 (0-4)
                   20 days or less: 7534 (0-4)
Conclusion: he runs best when fresh.
Summary of ideal conditions When running fresh (after a break of six weeks or more) his record reads: 58111 (3-5), improving to: 11 (2-2) over fences only. His four wins came over distances ranging from 2m-2m6f, the majority on good or faster going.

SILVERBURN (IRE)
7yo b g (P F Nicholls)
Race type   NHF: 21 (1-2)
                   Hdl: 21146 (2-5)
                   Chs: 2314 (1-4)
Conclusion: he's effective over hurdles and fences.
Distance   2m-2m2f: 2111 (3-4)
                   2m3f-2m5f: 2421 (1-4)
                   3m+: 634 (0-3)
Conclusion: all his wins have come at trips short of 3m.
Going   Good or faster: 26 (0-2)
                   Good to soft: 4234 (0-4)
                   Soft/heavy: 21111 (4-5)
Conclusion: he seems best on soft or heavy going.
Summary of ideal conditions When racing on soft or heavy going his record reads: 21111 (4-5), with the sole defeat by a short head on his racecourse debut. All his wins have come at 2m-2m5f but he has yet to encounter his preferred ground conditions when racing over 3m or further.

SIMON
9yo b g (J L Spearing)

Race type	Hdl: 1224273 (1-7)
	Ch: 434121152611F52U4U (5-18)
Conclusion:	he's best over fences.
Distance	2m-2m2f110y: 142 (1-3)
	2m3f-2m6f110y: 27343412 (1-8)
	3m+: 21152611F52U4U (4-14)
Conclusion:	he's best at 3m or further. His 2m5f Wincanton win (21 January 2006) was a most fortunate one as he was held in third place when left clear by two fallers.
Going	Good or faster: 4F524U (0-6)
	Good to soft: 715U (1-4)
	Soft: 122234312611 (4-12)
	Heavy: 421 (1-3)
Conclusion:	he's best on good to soft or softer going.
Fresh	Seasonal debuts: 1455 (1-4)
Conclusion:	he won on his racecourse debut in Ireland when trained by Philip Fenton but has finished well beaten in three reappearance efforts for current trainer John Spearing.
Track (chase starts only)	
	Flat: 4341211511F4U (5-13)
	Significant undulations: 2652U (0-5)
Conclusion:	he seems best on flat tracks.

Summary of ideal conditions Combine chase starts with racing at 3m or further, outside of his seasonal debuts, and his record becomes: 112611F2U4U (4-11), improving to: 1111 (4-4) on flat tracks and on good to soft or softer going.

SIR FREDERICK (IRE)
8yo b g (W J Burke)

Race type	NHF: 64 (0-2)
	Hdl: 42U1P1715 (3-9)
	Chs: 426215P411P0P4 (3-14)
Conclusion:	he is effective over hurdles and fences.
Fresh (absence since last race)	
	35 days or longer: 6U1112410P (4-10)
	34 days or less: 442P7546215P1P4 (2-15)
Conclusion:	he runs especially well when fresh.

Distance	2m-2m2f: 6441 (1-4)
	2m3f-2m6f: 2UP17142621P411P4 (5-17)
	3m-3m1f: 550 (0-3)
	3m4f+: P (0-1)
Conclusion:	he seems best at trips short of 3m.
Field size	20 or more runners: 21511P (3-6)
	16-19 runners: 644116204 (2-9)
	12-15 runners: U42P (0-4)
	11 or fewer runners: P75P41 (1-6)
Conclusion:	he likes to come late off a strong pace and seems ideally served by big fields.

Summary of ideal conditions When running fresh (after a break of five weeks or longer) his record over hurdles or fences becomes: U1112410P (4-9), improving to: 1111 (4-4) in fields of 16 or more runners at trips short of 3m. His wins have come on ground ranging from good to firm through to soft.

SNOOPY LOOPY (IRE)
10yo ch g (P Bowen)

Race type	NHF: 1 (1-1)
	Hdl: 133391 (2-6)
	Chs: 2365312312B11 (4-13)
Conclusion:	he is effective over hurdles and fences.
Distance	2m-2m2f: 111 (3-3)
	2m3f-2m6f110y: 33936111 (3-8)
	2m7f110y-3m2f: 32531232 (1-8)
	4m+: B (0-1)
Conclusion:	his last three wins have come at trips short of 3m.
Going	Good to firm or faster: 22 (0-2)
	Good: 119632B1 (3-8)
	Good to soft: 335311 (2-6)
	Soft/heavy: 3131 (2-4)
Conclusion:	he seems effective on any going.
Headgear	Cheekpieces: 12312B11 (4-8)
	Without headgear: 113339123653 (3-12)
Conclusion:	his best recent efforts have come in cheekpieces.

Summary of ideal conditions When running in cheekpieces his record reads: 12312B11 (4-8), improving to: 111 (3-3) at 2m3f-2m6f110y.

SNOWY MORNING (IRE)
8yo b g (W P Mullins)

Race type	NHF: 1 (1-1)
	Hdl: 2111 (3-4)
	Chs: 121124F3332 (3-11)
Conclusion:	he's effective over hurdles and fences.
Going	Good or faster: 143 (1-3)
	Good to yielding: 2 (0-1)
	Yielding: 23 (0-2)
	Yielding to soft: 13 (1-2)
	Soft: F11 (2-3)
	Soft to heavy: 2 (0-1)
	Heavy: 2111 (3-4)
Conclusion:	he runs especially well in the mud.

Summary of ideal conditions He has only once finished out of the first three places when completing the course and is effective over a variety of trips – winning over 2m2f early last season before his Grand National third. His form figures can be improved to: 21211F11 (5-8) when only considering his runs on soft or heavy going.

SOU'WESTER
8yo b g (C L Tizzard)

Race type	Hdl: 6005213221 (2-10)
	Chs: 54F13P31111 (5-11)
Conclusion:	he's effective over hurdles and fences.
Distance	2m-2m1f: 6552211111 (5-10)
	2mf110y-2m5f: 0024F113P3 (2-10)
	2m6f: 3 (0-1)
Conclusion:	he seems best at about 2m.
Trainer	B J Llewellyn: 60 (0-2)
	R Flint: 05254F (0-6)
	C Roberts: 1 (1-1)
	C L Tizzard: 322113P31111 (6-12)
Conclusion:	he has improved since joining current trainer Colin Tizzard.

Summary of ideal conditions Since the start of 2006 he has a record of: 1322113P31111 (7-13), improving to: 2211111 (5-7) at 2m-2m2f. He has won on ground ranging from fast through to soft and seems happiest on flat/sharp tracks such as Wincanton.

SPACE COWBOY (IRE)
8yo b g (G L Moore)

Race type	Hdl: F253326339U8801511F868701 (4-25)
	Chs: 42126233 (1-8)
Conclusion:	he's effective over hurdles and fences.
Going	Good to firm or faster: 2201511016 (4-10)
	Good: 533698F88742133 (1-15)
	Good to soft: F3822 (0-5)
	Soft/heavy: 3U6 (0-3)
Conclusion:	he's best on fast ground.
Course	Fontwell: 6311F13 (3-7)
	Newton Abbot: 511 (2-3)
	Others: F2533239U88086870422623 (0-23)
Conclusion:	he has yet to win away from Fontwell or Newton Abbot.

Summary of ideal conditions When racing on good to firm or faster going his record is: 2201511016 (4-10), improving to: 15111 (4-5) when racing at Fontwell or Newton Abbot only.

SQUIRES LANE (IRE)
9yo b g (Andrew Turnell)

Race type	Chs: 65216PPP116U (3-12)
Conclusion:	all his runs have taken place over fences.
Field size	12 or more runners: 65U (0-3)
	10-11 runners: 2PPP (0-4)
	8-9 runners: 616 (1-3)
	7 or fewer runners: 11 (2-2)
Conclusion:	all his wins have come in small fields.
Track	Left-handed: 216P1U (2-6)
	Right-handed: 65PP16 (1-6)
Conclusion:	he has won twice on left-handed tracks but has often earned the comment 'jumped right' and is likely to prove best right-handed.

Summary of ideal conditions When racing in single-figure line-ups his record reads: 16116 (3-5), improving to: 11 (2-2) in fields of seven or fewer runners only. He has winning form on ground ranging from good through to soft.

ST MATTHEW (USA)

10yo b g (Mrs S J Smith)

Race type Hdl: 1214F2213361946043 (4-18)
Ch: 1131FF8519F3106P8P64 (5-20)

Conclusion: he's effective over hurdles and fences.

Field size (chase starts only)

12 or more runners: 890P8P64 (0-8)
8-11 runners: 15F3 (1-4)
7 or fewer runners: 131FF116 (4-8)

Conclusion: all his chase wins have come in small fields.

Class 1 (Grade 1, 2 or 3): 33F9F604 (0-8)
1 (Listed): 81 (1-2)
2: 3F6519341P083P64 (2-16)
3: 4F22116 (2-7)
4 or lower: 12111 (4-5)

Conclusion: he has yet to win above Listed level.

Summary of ideal conditions When racing over fences in fields of seven or fewer runners, below Grade 3 level, his record becomes: 11F116 (4-6), improving to: 1F11 (3-4) on good to soft or softer going.

STAN (NZ)

9yo b g (Miss Venetia Williams)

Race type Hdl: 3241201640 (2-10)
Chs: 133P32U6F3725114 (3-16)

Conclusion: he's effective over hurdles and fences.

Field size 14 or more runners: 3210660F11 (3-10)
12-13 runners: 43 (0-2)
11 or fewer runners: 211433P32U7254 (2-14)

Conclusion: he sometimes pulls too hard and seems best suited to racing in large fields.

Time of year Jan: 232 (0-3)
Feb: 5 (0-1)
Mar: 02U (0-3)
Apr: 166114 (3-6)
May: 10 (1-2)
Jun-Sep: no runs
Oct: 3243F (0-5)
Nov: 433 (0-3)
Dec: 1P7 (1-3)

Conclusion: he tends to peak in the spring.

Headgear   Blinkers: 32U60F37 (0-8)
                      Without headgear: 324120161433P25114 (5-18)
Conclusion: he has yet to win when wearing headgear.
Summary of ideal conditions When racing over fences in fields of 12 or more
runners his record becomes: 6F311 (2-5), improving to: 11 (2-2) without headgear.
He is effective from 2m-2m5f and seems best when racing on good to soft or faster
going in the spring.

STANDIN OBLIGATION (IRE)

9yo ch g (P Monteith)
Race type   Hdl: 11111P01 (6-8)
                      Chs: 11133P40231P (4-12)
Conclusion: he has winning form over hurdles and fences.
Time of year   April to mid-November: 111111111P1P (10-12)
                      Other months: P0334023 (0-8)
Conclusion: he has a strong seasonal pattern to his form.
Track   Left-handed: 111P0111133P40231 (8-17)
                      Right-handed: 11P (2-3)
Conclusion: he won twice on right-handed tracks over hurdles but earned the
                      comment "jumped left" when pulled up in a handicap chase at
                      right-handed Perth last season.
Class   Grade 1: no runs
                      Grade 2: P (0-1)
                      Grade 3: no runs
                      Listed: 1040 (1-4)
                      Class 2 or lower: 1111P111133231P (9-15)
Conclusion: the majority of his wins have come below Pattern class.
Summary of ideal conditions When racing in Class 2 or lower company his
record reads: 1111P111133231P (9-15), improving to: 111111111 (9-9) if we only
consider his runs from April to mid-November and throw out his chase starts on
right-handed tracks.

STARZAAN (IRE)

9yo b g (H Morrison)

Race type	Hdl: 41044243310543770 (2-17)
	Chs: 11P61 (3-5)
Conclusion:	he's effective over hurdles and fences.
Distance	2m-2m2f: 4104444 (1-7)
	2m3f-2m6f: 23105111 (4-8)
	3m+: 33770P6 (0-7)
Conclusion:	he doesn't seem to stay 3m.

Field size (hurdles starts only)

- 12 or more runners: 41044430770 (1-11)
- 10-11 runners: 5 (0-1)
- 8-9 runners: 143 (1-3)
- 7 or fewer runners: 23 (0-2)

Field size (chase starts only)

- 12 or more runners: no runs:
- 10-11 runners: P (0-1)
- 8-9 runners: 6 (0-1)
- 7 or fewer runners: 111 (3-3)

Conclusion: his was not a fluent jumper of hurdles, his only big-field success coming when odds-on for a Folkestone maiden, and it's a similar story over fences – his three wins coming in fields of just five, two and five runners.

Summary of ideal conditions When racing from 2m3f-2m6f his record becomes: 23105111 (4-8), improving to: 111 (3-3) in chases of seven or fewer runners only.

STORM OF APPLAUSE (IRE)

7yo b g (P J Hobbs)

Race type	NHF: 5 (0-1)
	Hdl: 5368213 (1-7)
	Chs: 4432212 (1-7)
Conclusion:	he's effective over hurdles and fences.
Going	Good to firm or faster: 14 (1-2)
	Good: 55682342212 (1-11)
	Good to soft: 33 (0-2)
	Soft/heavy: no runs
Conclusion:	he has avoided soft or heavy going throughout his career.

Track	Left-handed: 5621422 (1-7)
	Right-handed: 53834321 (1-8)
Conclusion:	although a narrow winner at right-handed Ludlow last term he jumped out to his left that day and is likely to prove best on left-handed tracks.

Summary of ideal conditions Combine left-handed hurdle or chase starts with running on good or faster going and his record becomes: 621422 (1-6). Given his tendency to make jumping errors, small fields are likely to suit best.

STRAWBERRY (IRE)
7yo b m (J W Mullins)

Race type	NHF: 2427 (0-4)
	Hdl: 2P3101836 (2-9)
	Chs: P52221 (1-6)
Conclusion:	she's effective over hurdles and fences.
Time of year	Jan-Feb: 362 (0-3)
	Mar-Apr: 242101821 (3-9)
	May-Oct: no runs
	Nov-Dec: 72P3P52 (0-7)
Conclusion:	all her wins have come in the spring.

Summary of ideal conditions When racing over hurdles or fences during the months of March and April her record becomes: 101821 (3-6), with the wins coming at odds of 20-1, 5-4 and 14-1. She has winning form on both fast and soft going.

STRIPE ME BLUE
6yo b g (P J Jones)

Race type	NHF: 2021 (1-4)
	Hdl: F5F26217 (1-8)
Conclusion:	he had useful form in bumpers and has recorded one 16-1 success from eight tries over hurdles.
Distance	2m-2m2f: 2021262 (1-7)
	2m3f-2m5f: F5F (0-3)
	2m6f+: 17 (1-2)
Conclusion:	he is effective over a variety of trips.
Going	Good or faster: 227 (0-3)
	Good to soft: 0FF2621 (1-7)
	Soft: 5 (0-1)
	Heavy: 1 (1-1)
Conclusion:	he seems happiest on good to soft or softer going.

Field size	12 or more runners: 20227 (0-5)
	11 or fewer runners: 21F5F61 (2-7)
Conclusion:	he's a front-runner and is best able to dominate when racing in small fields.
Fresh	Seasonal debuts: 20F (0-3)
Conclusion:	he might need his first run of the season.

Summary of ideal conditions When racing in fields of 11 or fewer runners, outside of his seasonal debuts, his record becomes: 21F561 (2-6). He won a bumper at stiff/undulating Exeter but his best efforts over hurdles have come on flat tracks.

SUPER JUDGE (IRE)
6yo b g (M Sheppard)

Race type	NHF: P46 (0-3)
	Hdl: 76405030890 (0-11)
	Chs: 42U1F71PUUU (2-11)
Conclusion:	he's best over fences.
Field size (chase starts only)	
	12 or more runners: 42F7P (0-5)
	10-11 runners: U (0-1)
	8-9 runners: U1UU (1-4)
	7 or fewer runners: 1 (1-1)
Conclusion:	he seems best in small fields.

Summary of ideal conditions When racing over fences in fields of nine or fewer runners his record is: U11UU (2-5), with both wins coming over 3m1f110y on fast ground at Hereford.

SUPREME CARA
8yo b m (C J Down)

Race type	NHF: 4831 (1-4)
	Hdl: 3431 (1-4)
	Chs: 2365F (0-5)
Conclusion:	she has yet to win over fences but was only beaten by a head on her chase debut.
Distance	2m-2m2f: 483 (0-3)
	2m2f110y-2m5f: 13432 (1-5)
	3m+: 1365F (1-5)
Conclusion:	she improved for the step up beyond 2m2f.

Going	Good or faster: 45 (0-2)
	Good to soft: 82 (0-2)
	Soft: 1336F (1-5)
	Heavy: 3341 (1-4)
Conclusion:	she needs good to soft or slower going.
Track	Left-handed: 4831343125 (2-10)
	Right-handed: 36F (0-3)
Conclusion:	she has yet to score on a right-handed track.
Course	Ascot: 6 (0-1)
	Bangor: 2 (0-1)
	Chepstow: 83 (0-2)
	Exeter: 3F (0-2)
	Fontwell: 1 (1-1)
	Lingfield: 5 (0-1)
	Warwick: 3341 (1-4)
	Worcester: 4 (0-1)
Conclusion:	her best efforts have come on sharp tracks.
Class	1: 46 (0-2)
	2: no runs
	3: 13 (1-2)
	4 or lower: 48313325F (1-9)
Conclusion:	she has yet to win above Class 3 level.

Summary of ideal conditions When racing on good to soft or softer going her record reads: 8313431236F (2-11), improving to: 13312 (2-5) when racing left-handed below Class 1 level.

SURFACE TO AIR

7yo b g (C C Bealby)

Race type	Hdl: 3521PP (1-6)
	Chs: 2111 (3-4)
Conclusion:	he's best over fences.
Distance	2m5f-2m6f110y: 321PP2 (1-6)
	3m-3m1f: 5 (0-1)
	3m4f+: 111 (3-3)
Conclusion:	he is effective at about 2m6f but improved for the step up to 3m4f+ last term.
Going	Good to firm or faster: 1 (1-1)
	Good: 311 (2-3)
	Good to soft: 21 (1-2)
	Soft: 52P (0-3)
	Heavy: P (0-1)
Conclusion:	he prefers good to soft or faster going.

Track   Left-handed: 5111 (3-4)
                    Right-handed: 321PP2 (1-6)
Conclusion: he seems effective on any track.
Summary of ideal conditions When racing over fences his record is: 2111 (3-4), with the sole defeat by a neck over an inadequate 2m6f110y trip.

TAMARINBLEU (FR)
8yo b g (D E Pipe)
Distance   2m-2m2m110y: 123918204251917 (4-15)
                    2m3f-2m5f110y: 0261P13 (2-7)
                    3m+: 631 (1-3)
Conclusion: he is effective over a variety of trips.
Going   Good to firm or faster: no runs
                    Good: 900241P6313 (2-11)
                    Good to soft: 218296117 (3-9)
                    Soft/heavy: 13251 (2-5)
Conclusion: he seems happiest on good to soft or softer going.
Fresh (absence since last race)
                    84 days or longer: 1126P1 (3-6)
                    43-83 days: 3997 (0-4)
                    35-42 days: 811 (2-3)
                    28-34 days: 5131 (2-4)
                    27 days or less: 20202463 (0-8)
Conclusion: he runs especially well when fresh – all his wins have come after a break of at least four weeks and he has a 50% strike-rate when rested for 12 weeks or more.
Track   Left-handed: 2908202259663173 (1-16)
                    Right-handed: 131411P11 (6-9)
Conclusion: he has a superior strike-rate on right-handed tracks.
Summary of ideal conditions When running fresh (after a break of four weeks or longer) his record becomes: 13918251961P31117 (7-17), improving to: 13111P11 (6-8) on right-handed tracks.

THAT LOOK

5yo b g (D E Cantillon)

Race type	Hdl: 12416115 (4-8)
	Chs: 114 (2-3)
Conclusion:	he is effective over hurdles and fences.
Going	Good to firm or faster: 1241111 (5-7)
	Good: 1465 (1-4)
	Good to soft or softer: no runs
Conclusion:	he has only raced on good or faster going.
Track	Left-handed: 244 (0-3)
	Right-handed: 11116115 (6-8)
Conclusion:	he has a good record on right-handed tracks.

Summary of ideal conditions When racing over hurdles or fences his record is: 12411146115 (6-11), improving to: 11116115 (6-8) on right-handed tracks only.

THE BANDIT (IRE)

11yo b g (Miss E C Lavelle)

Race type	NHF: 7 (0-1)
	Hdl: 8F62816355 (1-10)
	Ch: 11P2342PFP8501PP8148P (4-21)
Conclusion:	he's effective over hurdles and fences.
Going	Good to firm or faster: 211P1 (3-5)
	Good: 7886P2343PP808458P (0-18)
	Good to soft: F61255 (1-6)
	Soft/heavy: 1PP (1-3)
Conclusion:	he is suited by fast ground.
Class	1: P (0-1)
	2: 23PPP80P8 (0-9)
	3: F861142351P81455P (4-17)
	4 or lower: 78621 (1-5)
Conclusion:	he has yet to win above Class 3 company.
Field size (chase starts only)	
	12 or more runners: 22P508P (0-7)
	11 or fewer runners: 11P34PP81PP814 (4-14)
Conclusion:	his chase wins have come in small fields (eight, four, nine and six ran).

Summary of ideal conditions Combine small-field (11 or fewer runners) chase starts with running in Class 3 or lower company and his record becomes: 1141P14 (4-7), improving to: 11 (2-2) on good to firm or faster going.

THE LISTENER (IRE)

9yo gr g (R H & Mrs S Alner)

Race type	NHF: 5 (0-1)
	Hdl: 04F121S (2-7)
	Chs: 111FF2120U1315 (6-14)
Conclusion:	he has winning form over hurdles and fences.
Going	Good or faster: 54FU (0-4)
	Good to yielding: 3 (0-1)
	Good to soft: S11205 (2-6)
	Yielding to soft: 1 (1-1)
	Soft: 011 (2-3)
	Heavy: F21F121 (3-7)
Conclusion:	he needs slow going.
Field size	12 or more runners: 50FSF0 (0-6)
	8-11 runners: 411115 (4-6)
	7 or fewer runners: 2111F212U3 (4-10)
Conclusion:	he's best in small fields.

Summary of ideal conditions When racing in fields of 11 or fewer runners on good to soft or softer going his record is: 121111F212115 (8-13). These figures can be improved slightly to: 1211F1211 (6-9) if we only consider the runs on yielding to soft or softer ground.

THE LUDER (IRE)

7yo b g (P F Nicholls)

Race type	Hdl: 4221317 (2-7)
	Chs: 1U2423P1 (2-8)
Conclusion:	he's effective over hurdles and fences.
Distance	2m-2m2f: 42 (0-2)
	2m3f-2m5f110y: 2 (0-1)
	2m6f-2m6f110y: 131724 (2-6)
	3m+: 1U23P1 (2-6)
Conclusion:	he needs at least 2m6f, preferably 3m or further.
Going	Good or faster: 71 (1-2)
	Good to soft: 4211U2 (2-6)
	Soft/heavy: 231243P (1-7)
Conclusion:	the majority of his wins have come on good to soft or faster going.

Summary of ideal conditions Combine a distance of 3m or further with racing on good to soft or faster going and his record becomes: 1U21 (2-4).

THE REAL DEAL (IRE)

7yo b g (Nick Williams)

Race type	Non-handicap hurdles: 0421 (1-4)
	Handicap hurdles: 0160 (1-4)
	Non-handicap chases: F5P4 (0-4)
	Handicap chases: P11U (2-4)
Conclusion:	he is effective over hurdles and fences.
Distance	2m-2m1f: 420 (0-3)
	2m2f-2m5f: 0160F1U (2-7)
	3m+: 15P4P1 (2-6)
Conclusion:	he is effective at about 2m4f but seems best at 3m.
Going	Good or faster: 4F5PU (0-5)
	Good to soft: 02016411 (3-8)
	Soft: 1P (1-2)
	Heavy: 0 (0-1)
Conclusion:	he's best on good to soft or softer going.
Fresh (absence since last race)	
	42 days or longer: 0421F1 (2-6)
	35-41 days: 01 (1-2)
	28-34 days: 41 (1-2)
	27 days or less: 605PPU (0-6)
Conclusion:	he runs well when fresh, all his wins coming after a break of at least four weeks.

Summary of ideal conditions When running fresh (after a break of at least four weeks) his record becomes: 042011F411 (4-10), improving to: 111 (3-3) in handicap company only.

THE RISKY VIKING (IRE)

9yo b g (Nick Williams)

Race type	Hdl: 24224 (0-5)
	Chs: P81F565 (1-7)
Conclusion:	he's best over fences.
Distance	2m6f-3m1f: 22485 (0-5)
	3m2f-3m5f: P42F5 (0-5)
	4m+: 16 (1-2)
Conclusion:	he improved for the step up to 4m.
Going	Good or faster: 8 (0-1)
	Good to soft: P265 (0-4)
	Soft: 4241F (1-5)
	Heavy: 25 (0-2)
Conclusion:	he is suited by soft or heavy going.

Fresh   Seasonal debuts: P8 (0-2)
Conclusion: he is likely to need his first run of the season.
Summary of ideal conditions When racing on soft or heavy going his record
becomes: 24241F5 (1-7), improving to: 421F (1-4) at 3m2f or further.

THEATRE DIVA (IRE)
7yo b m (Miss Venetia Williams)
Race type   NHF: 20947 (0-5)
                       Hdl: 250243237641202121 (3-18)
                       Chs: 121BU (2-5)
Conclusion: she took a while to break her duck but has now won five of her
                   last 12 starts.
Trainer   D T Hughes: 2094725024323764 (0-16)
                       H D Daly: 1202121 (3-7)
                       Miss Venetia Williams: 121BU (2-5)
Conclusion: she has a good record since arriving in Britain from Ireland.
Track (UK runs only)
                       Left-handed: 20BU (0-4)
                       Right-handed: 12121121 (5-8)
Conclusion: she runs especially well on right-handed tracks.
Field size (chase runs only)
                       12 or more runners: BU (0-2)
                       11 or fewer runners: 121 (2-3)
Conclusion: she has yet to complete the course when racing over fences in a
                   big field.
Summary of ideal conditions When racing right-handed in the UK her record
reads: 12121121 (5-8).

THREE MIRRORS
8yo b g (Ferdy Murphy)
Race type   Hdl: 75156124 (2-8)
                       Chs: 86822221131406P21 (4-17)
Conclusion: he's best over fences.
Distance (chase starts only)
                       2m-2m2f: 8683P (0-5)
                       2m3f-2m5f: 22211141 (4-8)
                       2m6f+: 2062 (0-4)
Conclusion: all his chase wins have come at about 2m4f but he does stay
                   further.

Going (chase starts only)

Good to firm or faster: 2114 (2-4)

Good: 8202 (0-4)

Good to yielding: 6 (0-1)

Good to soft: 221P1 (2-5)

Soft/heavy: 86 (0-2)

Conclusion: he's best on good to soft or faster going.

Track (chase starts only)

Left-handed: 622211406P21 (3-12)

Right-handed: 88213 (1-5)

Conclusion: his right-handed win came when 2-9 favourite and his trainer believes him best suited to racing left-handed.

Field size (chase starts only)

12 or more runners: 8682202 (0-7)

10-11 runners: 23 (0-2)

8-9 runners: 26P1 (1-4)

7 or fewer runners: 1114 (3-4)

Conclusion: all his chase wins have come in single-figure fields.

Summary of ideal conditions Combine chase starts at 2m3f or further with racing on good to soft or faster going and his record becomes: 22221114021 (4-11), improving to: 2114 (2-4) on good to firm or faster going, with both defeats coming first time out.

TIDAL BAY (IRE)

7yo b g (J Howard Johnson)

Race type   NHF: 22 (0-2)

Hdl: 111221 (4-6)

Chs: 111211 (5-6)

Conclusion: he has yet to finish worse than second during his career.

Going   Good to firm or faster: 2 (0-1)

Good: 1111 (4-4)

Good to soft: 2211 (2-4)

Soft: 11 (2-2)

Heavy: 212 (1-3)

Conclusion: he seems effective under most conditions.

Summary of ideal conditions Quite simply he has yet to run a bad race, recording figures of: 22111221111211 (9-14), improving to: 111211 (5-6) when racing over fences for current trainer Howard Johnson, with the sole defeat by a neck after he made a bad blunder.

TIGER CRY (IRE)

10yo b g (A L T Moore)

Race type	NHF: 4 (0-1)
	Hdl: 2221220122460 (2-13)
	Chs: 34631232FPP31 (2-13)
Conclusion:	he's effective over hurdles and fences.
Distance	2m-2m2f: 422212236013212322FP4361 (4-24)
	2m4f-2m5f: 4P0 (0-3)
Conclusion:	he's best at about 2m.
Going	Good or faster: 12122F4P3 (2-9)
	Good to yielding: 430 (0-3)
	Yielding: 20231 (1-5)
	Yielding to soft: 226 (0-3)
	Soft: 23461P (1-6)
	Heavy: 2 (0-1)
Conclusion:	he performs best on fast ground.
Time of year	Mar-Oct: 422132122F4P10 (3-14)
	Nov-Feb: 2221346023P36 (1-13)
Conclusion:	three of his four wins came during the period of March to October, the other on 29 February.

Summary of ideal conditions Combine chases starts at 2m-2m2f with racing on yielding or faster going and his record becomes: 31232F31 (2-8), improving to: 312F1 (2-5) during the period of March to October only.

TOM SAYERS (IRE)

10yo b g (P J Hobbs)

Race type	NHF: 0 (0-1)
	Hdl: 07225F25481 (1-11)
	Chs: 66111F253F98121227123 (6-21)
Conclusion:	he is effective over hurdles and fences.
Going	Good to firm or faster: 4121 (2-4)
	Good: 1F253912712 (3-11)
	Good to soft: 02258661F82 (1-11)
	Soft/heavy: 0725F13 (1-7)
Conclusion:	he prefers good or faster going.

Time of year   Jan-Feb: 05F8668 (0-7)
                      Mar-May: 0254111F121 (5-11)
                      Jun-Aug: 221 (1-3)
                      Sep-Oct: 2571 (1-4)
                      Nov-Dec: 7223F923 (0-8)
Conclusion: he has a poor record during the winter months.
Summary of ideal conditions When racing over fences from March to October his record becomes: 111F251212271 (6-13).

TOM'S TOYBOX
6yo b g (C Grant)

Race type   NHF: 625 (0-3)
                      Hdl: 435564 (0-6)
                      Chs: 414421S11 (4-9)
Conclusion: he improved for the switch to fences.
Distance   2m-2m2f: 62544144421S11 (4-14)
                      2m3f-2m5f: 356 (0-3)
                      3m+: 5 (0-1)
Conclusion: he's best at about 2m.
Going   Good or faster: 6554421S11 (3-10)
                      Good to soft: 314 (1-3)
                      Soft: 245 (0-3)
                      Heavy: 64 (0-2)
Conclusion: he's best on fast going.
Headgear   Blinkers: 1444 (1-4)
                      Cheekpieces: 21S11 (3-5)
                      Without headgear: 625435564 (0-9)
Conclusion: all his wins have come when wearing headgear.
Summary of ideal conditions Combine chase starts at 2m-2m2f with running on good to soft or faster going and his record becomes: 14421S11 (4-8), improving to: 21S11 (3-5) when wearing cheekpieces.

TOP DRESSING (IRE)
7yo br g (J Howard Johnson)

Race type	NHF: 384 (0-3)
	Hdl: 0412 (1-4)
	Chs: 3116U2 (2-6)
Conclusion:	he's effective over hurdles and fences.
Distance	2m-2m2f: 38441116 (3-8)
	2m3f-2m5f: 023U2 (0-5)
Conclusion:	all his wins have come at about 2m.
Going	Good to firm: 2 (0-1)
	Good: 331 (1-3)
	Good to soft: 0412 (1-4)
	Soft: 84 (0-2)
	Heavy: 16U (1-3)
Conclusion:	he seems best with cut in the ground.
Fresh (absence since last race)	
	Seasonal debuts: 343 (0-3)
Conclusion:	he might need his first race of the season.

Summary of ideal conditions When racing over hurdles or fences, outside of his seasonal debuts, his record becomes: 0412116U2 (3-9), improving to: 116 (2-3) when racing over fences only at trips short of 2m3f.

TRIGGER THE LIGHT
7yo ch g (A King)

Race type	NHF: 384 (0-3)
	Hdl: 12216 (2-5)
	Chs: 11 (2-2)
Conclusion:	he's unbeaten over fences.
Distance	2m-2m2f110y: 384 (0-3)
	2m3f-2m6f: 1226 (1-4)
	3m+: 111 (3-3)
Conclusion:	he is unbeaten at 3m or further.
Going	Good or faster: no runs
	Good to soft: 321 (1-3)
	Soft/heavy: 8412161 (3-7)
Conclusion:	he seems best on soft or heavy going.

Fresh (absence since last race)

> 42 days or longer: 3111 (3-4)
> 35-41 days: 2 (0-1)
> 28-34 days: 4 (0-1)
> 27 days or less: 8216 (1-4)

Conclusion: he runs especially well when fresh.

Summary of ideal conditions When running fresh (after a break of six weeks or more) his record becomes: 3111 (3-4), with the sole defeat by less than three lengths when a 20-1 shot for his racecourse debut. A distance of 3m or further on soft or heavy going clearly suits.

TURKO (FR)

6yo gr g (P F Nicholls)

Race type	Hdl: 1221652 (2-7)
	Chs: 11217PP123F (4-11)
Conclusion:	he's effective over hurdles and fences.
Going	Good to firm or faster: P (0-1)
	Good: 165211PF (3-8)
	Good to soft: 221713 (2-6)
	Yielding to soft: 2 (0-1)
	Soft/heavy: 21 (1-2)
Conclusion:	his three good-ground wins came when favourite for weak events and he might prove best on good to soft or softer going.
Track	Aintree (Mildmay): 51P (1-3)
	Aintree (National): F (0-1)
	Cheltenham: 226273 (0-6)
	Chepstow: 2 (0-1)
	Fontwell: 1 (1-1)
	Leopardstown: 2 (0-1)
	Newbury: 1 (1-1)
	Sandown: 1 (1-1)
	Wetherby: P (0-1)
	Wincanton: 11 (2-2)
Conclusion:	he has a moderate record at Cheltenham and seems happiest on flat tracks such as Newbury and Wincanton.

Class	Grade 1: 265723 (0-6)
	Grade 2: 12PP (1-4)
	Grade 3: F (0-1)
	Others: 1212111 (5-7)

Conclusion: he has yet to score in Grade 1 company.

Field size (chase starts only)

	12 or more runners: 7F (0-2)
	8-11 runners: P23 (0-3)
	7 or fewer runners: 1121P1 (4-6)

Conclusion: he has yet to win a big-field chase.

Summary of ideal conditions His UK record below Grade 1 company stands at: 12121121PP1F (6-12) These figures can be improved to: 111111 (6-6) if we knock out the Cheltenham runs, those on fast ground and his chase starts in fields of 12 or more runners.

TWIST MAGIC (FR)
6yo b g (P F Nicholls)

| **Race type** | Hdl: 615P3 (1-5) |
| | Chs: 12F111261 (5-9) |

Conclusion: he's best over fences.

Going	Good or faster: P111 (3-4)
	Good to soft: 15126 (2-5)
	Soft: 63F12 (1-5)
	Heavy: no runs

Conclusion: he's best on good or faster going.

Summary of ideal conditions When racing over fences on good or faster going his record reads: 111 (3-3). He won the 2007 Tingle Creek on soft going but that was a slowly run affair and he has subsequently struggled to last home on anything other than good ground.

UNDERWRITER (USA)
8yo b g (M G Quinlan)

Race type Hdl: 310 (1-3)

Ch: U1F43043PF323 (1-13)

Conclusion: he's effective over hurdles and fences.

Distance 2m-2m2f110y: 30 (0-2)

2m3f-2m5f1`0y: 1UF (1-3)

3m+: 1F43043P323 (1-11)

Conclusion: his 2m4f win came over hurdles and he's likely to prove best at 3m+.

Track Left-handed: UF03 (0-4)

Right-handed: 31014343PF32 (2-12)

Conclusion: he has yet to win on a left-handed track.

Fresh First two runs after a long break (12 weeks+) or when rested for 5 weeks+: 31U13043PF323 (2-13)

Other runs: 0F3 (0-4)

Conclusion: he runs well when fresh.

Summary of ideal conditions When racing right-handed at 2m3f+ his record is: 114343PF32 (2-10), improving to: 11343PF32 (2-9) when fresh.

UNGARO (FR)
9yo b g (K G Reveley)

Race type NHF: 102 (1-3)

Hdl: 4F24311241656 (3-13)

Ch: 11166332F20 (3-11)

Conclusion: he has winning form over hurdles and fences.

Fresh First two runs each season or when rested for approximately five weeks+: 1024F1141611163620 (7-18)

Others runs: 2432563F2 (0-9)

Conclusion: he runs especially well when fresh.

Class Grade 1: 4516 (1-4)

Grade 2: 6 (0-1)

Grade 3: 16F0 (1-4)

Listed: 2 (0-1)

Others: 1024F243112113632 (5-17)

Conclusion: he scored in Grade 1 company as a novice but doesn't seem up to that level these days.

Track Flat/easy: 1024F24315111662F2 (5-18)

Stiff/undulating: 124166330 (2-9)

Conclusion: his best recent efforts have come on flat tracks.

Summary of ideal conditions When running fresh (first two runs each season or after a break of about five weeks or more) his record reads: 1024F1141611163620 (7-18). Since the start of the 2005/2006 season, these figures improve to: 11111662F2 (5-10) if we knock out his runs in Grade 1 company and those on stiff tracks (e.g. Carlisle, Cheltenham, Newcastle and Sandown).

VICTORY GUNNER (IRE)
10yo ch g (C Roberts)

Time of year	
	Jan: 96P419 (1-6)
	Feb: 5179436 (1-7)
	Mar: 220436 (0-6)
	Apr: 095PP (0-5)
	May-Sep: 59 (0-2)
	Oct: 68P7 (0-4)
	Nov: P31F3P7 (1-7)
	Dec: 8161514161 (5-10)

Conclusion: the majority of his wins have come in December.

Summary of ideal conditions He has peaked in late December in each of the last five seasons, winning over hurdles at Taunton (29 December 2003) and Chepstow (28 December 2004) before his hat-trick of chase wins in the Lincolnshire National (held at Market Rasen on Boxing Day) where he'll surely be heading again this year.

WENGER (FR)
8yo b g (S Lycett)

Race type	
	Hdl: P363512F803153495 (2-17)
	Chs: 212P243673571231 (3-16)

Conclusion: he's effective over hurdles and fences.

Time of year	
	Jan-Feb: 35395257 (0-8)
	Mar-May: P12F8412P21231 (4-14)
	Jun-Aug: 436 (0-3)
	Sep-Oct: 0 (0-1)
	Nov-Dec: 3631573 (1-7)

Conclusion: he tends to peak in the spring.

Trainer	
	P Winkworth: P363512F803153495212P2 (3-22)
	M Sheppard: 4367357 (0-7)
	S Lycett: 1231 (2-4)

Conclusion: he has improved since the switch to current trainer Shaun Lycett.

Summary of ideal conditions When racing during the period of March to May his record becomes: P12F8412P21231 (4-14), improving to: 1231 (2-4) for his current yard, with both wins coming on good or faster going at 2m4f or further.

WHISPERED SECRET (GER)
9yo b g (D E Pipe)

Race type	Hdl: 435214121557122 (4-15)
	Ch: 23112140U445743134P (4-19)
Conclusion:	he's effective over hurdles and fences.
Distance	2m-2m1f110y: 43P21425213 (2-11)
	2m2f-2m3f110y: 14 (1-2)
	2m4f-2m5f110y: 151312140413 (5-12)
	2m6f-2m7f: 2257 (0-4)
	3m+: 7U44P (0-5)
Conclusion:	he is best at trips short of 3m.
Going	Good or faster: 43P2141215712231121404574 (7-25)
	Good to soft: UP (0-2)
	Soft/heavy: 5431234 (1-7)
Conclusion:	the majority of his wins have come on good or faster but he seems to handle any going.
Track	Left-handed: 421411722311140U44574313 (7-24)
	Right-handed: 3P255122 (1-8)
Conclusion:	he has a superior strike-rate on left-handed tracks.
Field size	12 or more runners: 43P242150U2P (1-12)
	11 or fewer runners: 1157122311214445743134 (7-22)
Conclusion:	he's best in small fields.
Track	Tight: 32141255722114574 (4-17)
	Galloping: 4P1132140U431234P (4-17)
Conclusion:	although a multiple winner on tight tracks those victories were achieved in low-class races when returned at SPs of 4-7, 5-6, 4-5 and 5-6. He is likely to prove best on galloping tracks such as Cheltenham and Newbury.

Summary of ideal conditions When racing in fields of 11 or fewer runners his record becomes: 1157122311214445743134 (7-22).

WILD CANE RIDGE (IRE)
9yo gr g (L Lungo)

Race type	NHF: 11 (2-2)
	Hdl: 211418210 (4-9)
	Chs: 121F1264P2P (3-11)
Conclusion:	he is effective over hurdles and fences.
Distance	2m-2m3f: 11 (2-2)
	2m4f-2m7f: 21111211 (6-8)
	3m: 142F826P20 (1-10)
	3m4f+: 4P (0-2)
Conclusion:	he has a superior strike-rate at trips below 3m.
Going	Good or faster: 2P (0-2)
	Good to soft: 1280 (1-4)
	Soft: 1241121P (4-8)
	Heavy: 111F2641 (4-8)
Conclusion:	all his wins have come on slow going.
Class	1: 4640P (0-5)
	2: F12P2 (1-5)
	3: 21821 (2-5)
	4 or lower: 1121111 (6-7)
Conclusion:	he has yet to win in Class 1 company.

Summary of ideal conditions When racing in Class 2 or lower company his record is: 112111121F8212P21 (9-17), improving to: 1121111211 (8-10) at trips below 3m, with the latest defeat by a head.

WITHOUT A DOUBT
9yo b g (Carl Llewellyn)

Race type	NHF: 30268 (0-5)
	Hdl: 2212303975 (1-10)
	Ch: 1342526F5P2P4229 (1-16)
Conclusion:	he's effective over hurdles and fences.
Track	Left-handed: 30822753455PP (0-13)
	Right-handed: 261230391226F24229 (2-18)
Conclusion:	he has yet to win on a left-handed track.
Field size	12 or more runners: 30268097555PP9 (0-14)
	11 or fewer runners: 221233134226F2422 (2-17)
Conclusion:	he has yet to win in a big field.

Summary of ideal conditions When racing in small fields (11 or fewer runners) his record is: 221233134226F2422 (2-17), improving to: 12331226F2422 (2-13) on right-handed tracks.

WIZARD OF US

8yo b g (M Mullineaux)

Race type	Hdl: 91451317P78306810 (4-17)
Conclusion:	all his jumps runs have taken place over hurdles.
Distance	2m-2m2f: 91451317P830810 (4-15)
	2m3f-2m5f: 76 (0-2)
Conclusion:	he's best at about 2m.
Going	Good to firm or faster: no runs
	Good: 70681 (1-5)
	Good to soft: 183 (1-3)
	Soft: P70 (0-3)
	Heavy: 914513 (2-6)
Conclusion:	he is effective on good or softer going.
Field size	12 or more runners: 9117P30680 (2-10)
	11 or fewer runners: 4513781 (2-7)
Conclusion:	two of his wins came in big fields but, as a front-runner, he might prove best served by small line-ups.
Course	Aintree: 6 (0-1)
	Ayr: 0 (0-1)
	Cheltenham: P (0-1)
	Haydock: 45373 (0-5)
	Market Rasen: 10 (1-2)
	Stratford: 8 (0-1)
	Uttoxeter: 911178 (3-6)
Conclusion:	three of his four wins came at Uttoxeter, the other at Market Rasen.
Class	1: 57P00 (0-5)
	2: 118 (2-3)
	3: 473681 (1-6)
	4 or lower: 913 (1-3)
Conclusion:	he has yet to win in Class 1 company.

Summary of ideal conditions When racing over hurdles at 2m-2m2f in Class 2 or lower company his record becomes: 9141318381 (4-10), with the wins coming at odds of 40-1, 12-1, 9-1 and 20-1.

YOUR AMOUNT (IRE)

5yo b g (A King)

Race type	Hdl: 4031221 (2-7)
Conclusion:	all his jumps runs have taken place over hurdles.
Distance	2m-2m2f: 4031 (1-4)
	2m3f-2m5f: 221 (1-3)
Conclusion:	he improved for the step up beyond 2m2f.
Going	Good to firm or faster: no runs
	Good: 11 (2-2)
	Good to soft: 32 (0-2)
	Soft: 42 (0-2)
	Heavy: 0 (0-1)
Conclusion:	both his hurdle wins came on good ground but he has gone close on good to soft and soft going.
Track	Left-handed: 01221 (2-5)
	Right-handed: 43 (0-2)
Conclusion:	both his hurdle wins came on left-handed tracks (as did his two wins on the Flat) but it is too early to say that he can't act right-handed.

Summary of ideal conditions When racing over hurdles his record reads: 4031221 (2-7), improving to: 221 (1-3) at 2m3f or further. From left-to-right: 2nd — beaten by half-a-length (2m3f, soft), 2nd — beaten by a short head (2m4f, good to soft) and 1st (2m4f, good).

Glossary

Form Figures

1	First
2	Second
3	Third, etc
0	tenth or worse (sometimes referred to as a 'duck egg')
U	Unseated rider
P	Pulled-up
F	Fell
S	Slipped-up
R	Refused or ran out
B	Brought Down
C	Carried Out

The figures in brackets after a string of form figures represent the total wins/runs for a particular category. For example: Good to soft: 123U1 (2-5) – the horse in question has had five runs on good to soft going recording figures of first, second, third, unseated rider and first, a total of two wins from five runs.

Race type

NHF	National Hunt Flat race (also called bumpers) – a race for horses aged seven or under who have not run under any recognised Rules of Racing except in National Hunt Flat races in Great Britain or in Irish National Hunt Flat races
Hdl	Hurdle race
Chs	Chase (also referred to as a race 'over fences')

Distance

6f	Six furlongs (eight furlongs = one mile)
1m1f103y	One mile, one furlong and 103 yards (220 yards = one furlong)
2m	Two miles

Track

LH	Left-handed (the horses race in an anti-clockwise direction)
RH	Right-handed (the horses race clockwise)
F8	Figure-of-eight (the horses race both left-handed and right-handed)

Class

Pattern company	The collective term for Grade 1, 2, 3 and Listed races

Index

ACAMBO (GER) — Good to soft/faster going, fresh, preferably at 2m

AIR FORCE ONE (GER) — 2m4f+, second start onwards, preferably away from Cheltenham

ALBERTAS RUN (IRE) — 3m+, preferably on good or softer going

ALDERBURN — Chases, not seasonal debuts, preferably right-handed in small fields and on fast ground

ANDREAS (FR) — 2m, good or faster going, preferably in the spring

ARDAGHEY (IRE) — Fresh, preferably in a small field and below Class 1 level

BAGAN (FR) — 2m3f-2m5f, good or (preferably) good to soft going

BALLYFITZ — Hurdles below Grade 3 level, ideally at 3m+ on slow ground

BATTLECRY — Good to soft/faster going (preferably good/faster on a flat track)

BESHABAR (IRE) — All starts

BIBLE LORD (IRE) — Chases, preferably in a small field on good to soft/softer at 2m4f

BIG ROB (IRE) — Small-field chases, preferably on flat tracks below 3m and on fast ground

BLACK HILLS — Small-field chases, preferably right-handed and at trips below 3m

BLAEBERRY — 2m3f+, March-October, preferably below Class 1 level

BLANDINGS CASTLE — Newton Abbot handicaps, preferably at 2m

BRAVE VILLA (FR) — Chases of 11 or fewer runners, preferably at 2m on good to soft/softer and away from Wincanton

BRIERY FOX (IRE) — Fast ground, preferably in a small field

BRING ME SUNSHINE (IRE) — Small fields, ideally on good to soft/softer going at 2m-2m5f

BRONSON F'SURE — 3m+, good or faster going, preferably in the spring

CARIBOU (FR) — Good to soft/softer going (preferably soft/heavy), ideally on a right-handed track

CHARACTER BUILDING (IRE) — Good/softer going, ideally at 3m+

CLOUDY LANE — 2m4f+ (probably not stay 3m4f+), ideally from second start onwards and not on tight tracks

COACH LANE — 2m chases (consider over hurdles too), preferably in small fields on soft/heavy going

COPPER BAY (IRE) — Right-handed, good/faster going, preferably on a track with easy fences

CORNAS (NZ) — All starts

DANCING DASI (IRE) — Right-handed, good to soft or faster going

DICTUM (GER) — Soft or (preferably) heavy going, ideally on second start onwards

DOUBLE EAGLE — Right-handed, preferably on soft/heavy going at 2m-2m4f

DREAM ALLIANCE — Class 2 or lower, second start onwards, preferably at 2m4f-2m7f110y

EARTH PLANET (IRE) — Consider all starts but especially interesting in tongue-tie under Ruby Walsh

EDMO YEWKAY (IRE) — Small-field chases, preferably at 2m-2m3f on flat/galloping LH track

EL ZORRO — Fresh, preferably at 2m-2m5f on good to soft or softer going

ELUSIVE DREAM — Good/faster going, preferably in small fields.

ELVIS RETURNS — March to May, no headgear, preferably on good to soft/faster

ERIC'S CHARM (FR) — Right-handed tracks, excluding seasonal

FINGER ONTHE PULSE (IRE)	2m-2m5f, preferably from March to October when fresh
FOREST PENNANT (IRE)	2m3f+
FORGET THE PAST	2m4f-2m6f, yielding to soft or softer going, Grade 2 or lower company
FROM DAWN TO DUSK	Good to soft/faster, preferably at 2m6f or shorter from March-October
GONE TO LUNCH (IRE)	Hurdles, ideally on good or faster going
GREEN GAMBLE	Chases of 2m-2m1f, no headgear, ideally in small field and on sharp track
GUNGADU	Right-handed, preferably in a small field
GWANAKO (FR)	Left-handed, ideally on good or good to soft going
HALCON GENELARDAIS (FR)	2m6f+, good to soft/softer (preferably soft or heavy)
HELENS VISION	Fresh (six weeks+)
HENRY'S PRIDE (IRE)	Fresh (six weeks+), might prove best at about 3m on slow ground
HERMANO CORDOBES (IRE)	Chases, preferably on good/faster going and in small fields
HOWLE HILL (IRE)	Chases on good/faster going, preferably at 2m-2m3f on easy tracks
ICE BUCKET (IRE)	Right-handed chases, second start onwards, ideally on a flat track
IDLE TALK (IRE)	Class 2 or lower company, preferably in a small field at 3m+
IL DUCE (IRE)	Trips below 3m (preferably 2m4f), good to soft/faster going, ideally below Class 1 level
I'M SUPREME (IRE)	3m+, ideally on good or faster going
INCORPORATION	Soft/heavy going, cheekpieces, preferably at 2m when fresh
INGHWUNG	2m4f+, preferably on good to soft or faster going

IRISH RAPTOR (IRE)	3m+, good to soft softer, small fields
IRONSIDE (IRE)	Recent run, soft/heavy going, ideally in small field away from Warwick
JACK THE GIANT (IRE)	Good to soft or faster going, preferably in a small field when fresh
JIGSAW DANCER (IRE)	Handicaps, preferably right-handed on soft or heavy going
KALAHARI KING (FR)	All starts
KALCA MOME (FR)	2m-2m3f, soft or (preferably) heavy going, below Class 1 level
KEENAN'S FUTURE (IRE)	Left-handed chases, preferably in small fields on good to soft/softer going
KEMPSKI	Ayr hurdles, preferably on heavy going, in small fields and after a recent run
KENZO III (FR)	Fresh, especially first-time out
KILBEGGAN BLADE	Chases, good to soft or softer going, recent
KINGS EURO (IRE)	Good to soft/softer going, ideally at trips short of 3m
KINGS ROCK	Handicap hurdles, recent run, ideally at about 2m6f
KNIGHTON LAD (IRE)	3m+, preferably when fresh
KNOWHERE (IRE)	Fresh, preferably in small fields, below Grade 1 level at trips below 3m2f
LA VECCHIA SCUOLA (IRE)	2m hurdles, preferably in a small field on good or good to soft going
LENNON (IRE)	Good to soft/faster going, flat tracks, preferably at 2m
LODGE LANE (IRE)	Consider all starts but might prove best right-handed on slow ground
LORD HENRY (IRE)	Right-handed, preferably on fast ground below Class 1 level
LORD RYEFORD (IRE)	Fields of 11 or less, good or faster going

MADISON DU BERLAIS (FR) Chases, recent run, preferably on soft/heavy going and on a flat track

MAJAALES (USA) Handicap hurdles, preferably on good to soft/softer going at 2m-2m3f

MAJORCA 2m, fresh, preferably on fast ground

MALJIMAR (IRE) Fresh, preferably at about 2m4f

MANBOW (IRE) Chases of 2m4f+, good/faster ground, preferably at Wetherby

MASSINI SUNSET (IRE) Chases on good to soft/softer going, ideally in a big field

MASTER SEBASTIAN Races in January (consider in early February too), especially on soft/heavy going and at Ayr

MIGHTY MOOSE (IRE) Handicap chases, preferably on good or softer going at trips of about 2m4f

MIKO DE BEAUCHENE (FR) Left-handed, good to soft or softer going, preferably when fresh

MISSIS POTTS Consider all starts but most interesting below Class 1 level at about 2m

MISTER QUASIMODO 2m-2m6f (preferably 2m3f-2m6f), good to soft/softer going, ideally in small fields

MOKUM (FR) Chases on stiff tracks, second start onwards, ideally on good to soft/faster going

MON MOME (FR) Chases, good to soft/softer, not seasonal debuts, ideally below Class 1 level

MOON OVER MIAMI (GER) Left-handed, recent run

MOSSBANK (IRE) First two starts of the season (also consider after mid-season break)

MOTORWAY (IRE) Small fields (11 or fewer), preferably at 2m on good/softer going

MOUS OF MEN (FR) Consider all starts but likely to prove best over trips beyond 2m after a recent run

MR POINTMENT (IRE) Fresh, preferably left-handed on good to soft/softer going.

MY IMMORTAL	Good or faster going, preferably at 3m+ in a small field
NATAL (FR)	Flat tracks, ideally at 2m-2m5f110y
NENUPHAR COLLONGES (FR)	Consider all starts but ideally at 3m+, on slow going and on a stiff/galloping track
NEPTUNE COLLONGES (FR)	Small fields, preferably on slow going
NEVERTIKA (FR)	Chases of 2m3f+ (consider over shorter trips on slow going)
NOTANOTHERDONKEY (IRE)	Chases, first two runs each season, ideally at about 2m5f-2m6f on good/faster going
NUDGE AND NURDLE (IRE)	Right-handed
OAKFIELD LEGEND	Chases of 3m+ on good or faster going
OLD BENNY	3m+ (ideally 3m4f+), preferably on good to soft/softer going
OLLIE MAGERN	Small fields (nine or fewer), preferably on fast ground, left-handed and below Grade 1 level
O'MALEY (FR)	Fast ground, no headgear, preferably at 2m6f+ on a sharp track
OPENIDE	Small fields, yielding to soft/faster
OPERA MUNDI (FR)	Soft or heavy going, preferably at trips beyond 2m
PABLO DU CHARMIL (FR)	Small fields (preferably five or less)
PAN THE MAN (IRE)	Good/faster going, trips short of 2m5f, preferably in fields of seven or less in the spring/summer
PARSONS LEGACY (IRE)	Fresh, good to soft/faster going, preferably in small fields
PETITE MARGOT	Small fields, preferably at 2m6f+
POLITICAL PADDY	Consider all starts but especially interesting in cheekpieces on slow ground
PUNJABI	Hurdles, preferably on good or faster going
PUR DE SIVOLA (FR)	Right-handed

RACING DEMON (IRE)	Right-handed chases, below 3m
RASH MOMENT (FR)	Handicap chases of 2m3f-2m7f, very recent run, preferably on fast ground
REGAL HEIGHTS (IRE)	Recent run (within six weeks), good to soft/softer going, preferably below Class 1 level
RIMSKY (IRE)	Fresh, preferably without headgear on an undulating track
RING THE BOSS (IRE)	Consider all starts but ideally at 2m3f+ on slow going
ROLL ALONG (IRE)	Fresh, ideally on good to soft or softer going
ROMAN ARK	Soft or heavy going, preferably at 2m-2m4f
ROOKERY LAD	Left-handed chases, April to July
RUDIVALE (IRE)	2m3f+, good to soft or faster going
SAUNDERS ROAD (IRE)	Trips of about 2m4f
SCARLET MIX (FR)	Warwick
SERHAAPHIM	2m, good to soft/softer going, preferably at Plumpton
SILVER INNGOT (IRE)	Fresh, preferably on good or faster going
SILVERBURN (IRE)	Soft or heavy going
SIMON	3m+, second start onwards, preferably on a flat track and slow ground
SIR FREDERICK (IRE)	Fresh, preferably in big fields at around 2m4f-2m6f
SNOOPY LOOPY (IRE)	Cheekpieces, preferably at 2m3f-2m6f110y
SNOWY MORNING (IRE)	Consider all starts but especially interesting on soft or heavy going
SOU'WESTER	Consider all starts but especially interesting at 2m on flat/sharp tracks
SPACE COWBOY (IRE)	Good to firm or faster going, preferably at Fontwell or Newton Abbot
SQUIRES LANE (IRE)	Small fields

ST MATTHEW (USA)	Small-field chases, good to soft/softer
STAN (NZ)	Big fields, no headgear, ideally on good to soft/faster going in the spring
STANDIN OBLIGATION (IRE)	Class 2 or lower, preferably left-handed from April to mid-November
STARZAAN (IRE)	2m3f-2m6f, preferably over fences in a very small field
STORM OF APPLAUSE (IRE)	Left-handed, good or faster going, preferably in a small field
STRAWBERRY (IRE)	Spring
STRIPE ME BLUE	Small fields, second start onwards, preferably on flat tracks
SUPER JUDGE (IRE)	Small-field chases, preferably on fast ground
SUPREME CARA	Good to soft/softer going, 2m3f+, preferably below Class 1 level on sharp left-handed track
SURFACE TO AIR	Chases, preferably on good to soft/faster going and over marathon trips
TAMARINBLEU (FR)	Fresh, especially first time out, ideally on a right-handed track
THAT LOOK	Consider all starts but especially interesting right-handed on fast ground
THE BANDIT (IRE)	Small-field chases, Class 3 or lower, preferably on fast ground
THE LISTENER (IRE)	Small fields (11 or less), good to soft/softer (preferably soft/heavy)
THE LUDER (IRE)	3m+, good to soft or faster going
THE REAL DEAL (IRE)	Good to soft or softer going, fresh, preferably in handicaps at 3m+
THE RISKY VIKING (IRE)	Soft or heavy going, preferably over marathon trip on second start onwards
THEATRE DIVA (IRE)	Right-handed, preferably in a small field

THREE MIRRORS	Chases of 2m3f+, good to soft or faster going (preferably good to firm), ideally second start onwards on a left-handed track
TIDAL BAY (IRE)	All starts, possibly best left-handed on good to soft or softer going
TIGER CRY (IRE)	2m chases, good to soft or faster going, preferably from March to October
TOM SAYERS (IRE)	Chases, March-October, ideally on good or faster going
TOM'S TOYBOX	2m chases, good to soft or faster going, preferably when wearing cheekpieces
TOP DRESSING (IRE)	Second start onwards, preferably at about 2m
TRIGGER THE LIGHT	Fresh, preferably at 3m+ on soft or heavy
TURKO (FR)	Grade 2 or lower, preferably in small fields, on slow ground and away from Cheltenham
TWIST MAGIC (FR)	2m, good or faster going
UNDERWRITER (USA)	Right-handed tracks, preferably at 3m+ and when fresh
UNGARO (FR)	Fresh, preferably on flat/easy track and below Grade 1 level
VICTORY GUNNER (IRE)	Lincolnshire National, Market Rasen, Boxing Day
WENGER (FR)	Spring, preferably on good or faster going at 2m4f+
WHISPERED SECRET (GER)	Field of 11 or less, preferably on galloping left-handed tracks
WILD CANE RIDGE (IRE)	Class 2 or lower, preferably on good to soft/softer going
WITHOUT A DOUBT	Small fields (11 or fewer runners), preferably right-handed
WIZARD OF US	Good or softer going, 2m, Class 2 or lower, preferably in small fields at Uttoxeter
YOUR AMOUNT (IRE)	Hurdles, preferably at 2m3f+